Handbook for
First-
Managers

Managing
Effectively

Handbook for
*F*irst-Time
Managers

Managing
Effectively

Joseph & Susan Berk

Sterling Publishing Co., Inc.
New York

10   9   8   7   6   5   4   3   2   1

Published in 1998 by Sterling Publishing Company, Inc.
387 Park Avenue South, New York, N.Y. 10016
Originally published under the title *Managing Effectively:*
A Handbook for the First-Time Manager
© 1991 by Joseph and Susan Berk
Distributed in Canada by Sterling Publishing
% Canadian Manda Group, One Atlantic Avenue, Suite 105
Toronto, Ontario, Canada M6K 3E7
Distributed in Great Britain and Europe by Cassell PLC
Wellington House, 125 Strand, London WC2R 0BB, England
Distributed in Australia by Capricorn Link (Australia) Pty Ltd.
P.O. Box 6651, Baulkham Hills, Business Centre, NSW 2153, Australia
Manufactured in the United States of America

Sterling ISBN 0-8069-0678-2

Dedication

This book is dedicated to Martin Berk.

CONTENTS

INTRODUCTION

Unlike most management guides, this book focuses on the needs of new managers. Perhaps more significantly, both authors are working managers. The material presented in this book is not theoretical, nor is it based exclusively on the management hypotheses espoused in MBA programs (even though both authors hold MBAs). Rather, the concepts here come from three sources—management readings, observations of new managers in a variety of settings, and, predominantly, our own experiences.

Management is simultaneously an art and a science. The scientific aspects of the management discipline are fairly straightforward, and anyone with a reasonable degree of intelligence can learn the mechanics. We present these mechanics throughout the book, but we don't stop there. You can't be successful as a manager if you are equipped only with the rules and procedures of the managerial business. You have to be adept at the artistic side of the managerial discipline. This is the part that requires an appreciation of the essence of the manager's job: understanding what it is you are responsible for doing, determining the best way to do it, recruiting and cultivating the right people, and helping these people to realize their full potential.

This book is organized into four sections. We start out with the most basic management functions, and then move into more advanced concepts. The section on staffing and supervising, for example, offers guidance on how to develop your staff. The next section, on career building, explores several concepts that helped us to advance into and up through the management ranks. The final section discusses more global tasks, and examines how to conduct effective meetings, solve problems, and manage change, conflict, and risk.

Throughout this book, the emphasis is on the skills needed by new managers. We've been there. We know the uniqueness of the challenges one faces when attempting to make a successful transition from doing the work to managing it. No book can claim to offer a recipe for avoiding the mistakes that are an inevitable part of learning the management business, but we believe the suggestions offered in the following pages can greatly ease the transition.

Part I
BASIC FUNCTIONS

Chapter 1
PLANNING

Eileen Barzda paced the floor nervously. Eileen managed the communications group in a medium-sized apparel manufacturing company. The company's new line of fall clothing was about to be unveiled at a show Eileen had been working on for several weeks. Although the company held such conferences every year, Eileen had only recently been promoted to her current assignment, and it was the first time she had the responsibility for arranging the affair. Procurement representatives from every major retailer were seated in the crowd, and the show was about to begin.

Eileen's mind raced over the events of the last few days. She had spent many hours determining what the show should include, and what needed to be accomplished in order to bring it off in a professional manner. The show was an important one. If the buyers were not impressed, the fall line would not do well. Eileen was nervous not only because the show was important, but because it was also her first major project as a manager.

All of the refreshments had arrived on time and were attractively displayed where Eileen had designated. All the chairs were in place, and the modelling platform was set up. Eileen had checked the loudspeakers earlier, and everything worked properly. All of the models were changing into their outfits. One had called in sick earlier in the day, but Eileen had two backups lined up, and one arrived to take the vacant spot in plenty of time.

Eileen's mind ran through everything one more time. She was satisfied. All was ready. She walked onto the platform confidently, and began the introduction. The music started, and the first model walked out. Eileen described the outfit, the audience applauded, and the show proceeded flawlessly. Afterwards, the buyers enjoyed themselves at the refreshment counter. Several of them complimented Eileen, and told the other managers that the company could look forward to a very successful season. Many placed significant orders before they left. At the end of the show, after the last buyer had left, Mr. Jacobsen approached and complimented Eileen. Mr. Jacobsen owned the company, and his words carried a lot of weight.

"Very well done, Eileen. That was probably the best show we've ever had," he said.

"Thank you," Eileen replied.

"No, the thanks go to you," Jacobsen replied. "A lot of people will keep their jobs because of your success today. You must have spent a lot of time planning this."

"Yes, I did," Eileen said.

"Well, it showed. We need more of that around here."

With that, Jacobsen shook Eileen's hand, and turned to Eileen's boss. "You take care of her," he said. "She's one we want to keep."

***

Perhaps the best way to begin a book on management techniques for new managers is with a discussion on planning. Our experience shows that no other management skill is as important as the ability to plan. Our observations also show that it is an area ignored by many first-level managers, but actively practiced by middle managers, upper level managers, and successful business owners. We believe there's a message in this observation, and it's that unless the ability to plan is developed and mastered, progression beyond the first level of management is unlikely. Our experience further shows that failure is almost always tied to a lack of adequate planning. In other words, project and group failures are frequently the direct result of poor or non-existent planning. Just what is planning?

In this chapter, the focus will be on the planning skills needed for first-level management. The focus of first-level management is primarily on technical, project, and interpersonal issues (Figure 1–1). Strategic planning (i.e., charting future business areas and strategies) is a business necessity, but is not usually practiced nor required by new managers, and for that reason, won't be covered here.

To understand the need for sound planning practices at the first level of management, think about past business crises you've been involved with. Each crisis probably created a sense of urgency throughout the organization, with many people responding or being assigned to help fix the problem. When we've encountered such crises, a great deal of confusion and uncertainty surrounded the effort, particularly with respect to who was supposed to do what and by when in order to resolve the crisis. In such situations, few people seem to have a clear idea how to get from Point A (the crisis) to Point B (resolution of the crisis). In most cases not only is the path from Point A to Point B confused, but frequently Point B is also a subject of considerable mystery.

Taking the analysis a step further leads to a key question: What caused the crisis in the first place? Was it a dramatic change in the business environment, or was it simply caused by someone not meet-

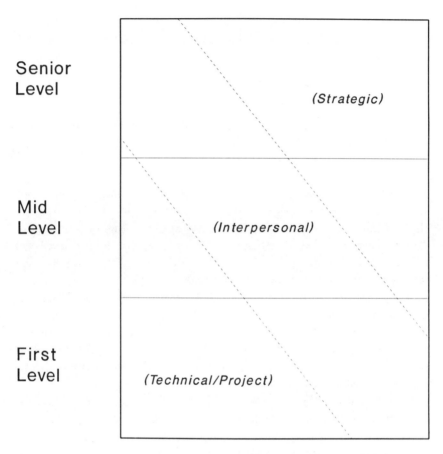

Senior
Level

(Strategic)

Mid
Level

(Interpersonal)

First
Level

(Technical/Project)

Figure 1–1. Management roles and practices. First-level management focuses on technical, project, and interpersonal issues.

ing a key commitment on time? And if it was the latter, did the person failing to meet the commitment know what he was supposed to do? In our experience, most crises are created by someone failing to meet a commitment either because of poor planning on their part, or because they were unaware of the requirement.

Eliminating these situations through the use of an approach that defines how to accomplish the objective is the purpose and essence of planning. Planning defines Point B, and describes how to get there. Our experience (as well as that of most other managers) shows that four steps are inherent to this process:

1. Identify the objective.
2. Identify all intermediate steps and resources necessary to allow a logical progression towards the objective.

3. Determine the sequence in which these steps must be performed.
4. Assign the appropriate people in order to assure task completion.

We've successfully used three planning methods to do this: the backwards planning method, the PERT method (PERT is an acronym for program evaluation and review technique), and the Gantt chart technique (named after H. L. Gantt, an industrial engineer whose planning methods achieved wide exposure during World War I). We feel (as do many managers) that the backwards planning and PERT methods offer distinct advantages over the Gantt chart method. Gantt charting is widely used, however, and for that reason will also be addressed later in this chapter.

THE BACKWARDS PLANNING METHOD

The backwards planning method is a conceptually simple technique developed and used extensively by the military. Backwards planning is ideal for planning simpler projects. The method starts with the desired result, or the objective, of the plan. The concept is to then back up in a sequential manner from the objective, identifying each required prior action (that's why it's called backwards planning). As each preceding task is identified, the time required to achieve it is estimated. The process continues, working backwards from each task, until all tasks are identified. Determining the starting date is then simple, as it merely requires adding the times required for each task.

This concept can be illustrated with a simple example. Suppose today is Tuesday, and your boss asks you to give a presentation in one week on the status of one of your projects. The boss has asked you to use viewgraphs, and to have hard copies of the presentation available for distribution after the presentation. The assignment sounds fairly simple, and one week to prepare seems more than adequate. The backwards planning method will be used to define what's necessary in order to be ready.

The first thing to identify is the objective. In this case, it's a project status review to be presented one week from today. Working backwards from this objective will be described here and shown in Figure 1–2. The first question is: What event should occur immediately prior to the presentation? A smooth presentation will require at least one or two rehearsals. If the presentation is targeted for thirty minutes, allowing three hours for the rehearsals seems reasonable. That means the presentation and the rehearsals will probably require one full day.

What should occur immediately prior to the rehearsal? Obviously, a room and an overhead projector will be needed. For the purposes of this example, assume your company requires one day's notice to reserve a room and a projector. That means another day will be needed for this.

If the room, the projector, and the time to rehearse and give the actual presentation are available, what else will be needed? You will need the viewgraph transparencies, along with hard copies to give to the audience. Since the art department requires one day to prepare these from the handwritten version, another day will be needed here.

Before the art department can begin its work, though, they will need a rough draft of the presentation. From prior experience, you know it will take you at least a day to gather the necessary information and prepare the rough draft. In order to be safe, it might be wise to allow two days for this activity.

If you've kept track of the time required, you can see that five days are necessary in order to be ready (as shown in Figure 1–2). Your boss told you to take a week to prepare, and if you don't want to work over the weekend, that means you have to start now. In our experience, that's one of the more interesting things about planning. If you don't plan your work, it always seems as though there's plenty of time to put

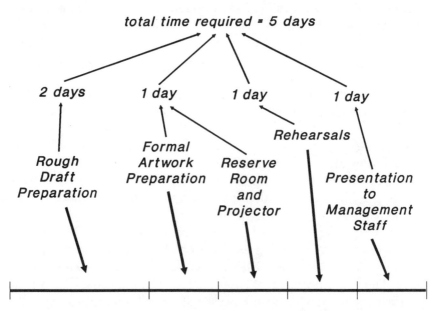

Figure 1–2. An illustration of the backwards planning method for a project status review. The process begins by identifying the objective, and works backwards to identify all preceding events.

off starting the project (but things usually get out of control as the completion date approaches). When you plan your work, just the opposite is true. Good planning shows the full extent of activities required prior to project completion, and this frequently shows that the required start date is sooner than you would otherwise expect.

THE PERT PLANNING METHOD

The PERT planning method was developed in the late 1950's to address the complexities of the Polaris missile program. The Polaris program required many highly sophisticated and technically complex engineering and manufacturing activities to occur at the proper time and in the proper sequence in order to meet cost and schedule requirements. The PERT method was created to assist in planning and controlling this sequence of events.

The PERT method is a formalized, graphical approach. Conceptually, it is a continuation of the backwards planning method (if you understand the backwards planning method, the wisdom inherent in the PERT method will be readily apparent). The PERT method goes several steps beyond the backwards planning method, though. It shows the time phasing and logical inter-relationships between tasks. Knowing this allows an identification of the total time required to complete a project. It also shows which parts of the project will pace the others (this is called the critical path, and will be discussed on page 16). Because the PERT method shows how one task leads into the next (in other words, the logical relationship of one task to another), it is very useful for making sure that all required tasks have been identified, and none have been left out.

These concepts can be illustrated with the same example used earlier for the backwards planning method. Like backwards planning, the PERT process begins by identifying the final objective of the project, which is to give a presentation one week from today. Figure 1–3 shows this as "Presentation to Management Staff," which is shown in a bubble on the right side of the chart. PERT practice is to work backwards from right to left, which allows reading the chart in the normal left-to-right manner. The same logic can be followed as in the previous example to identify each preceding event. These events are also shown on the PERT chart. Each bubble is connected by an arrow to the event it leads into, and the amount of time required to complete the task is shown underneath the arrow. The last step is to place the starting date for each task underneath its bubble.

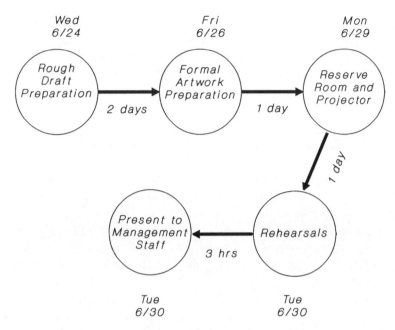

Figure 1–3. The PERT planning method for a project status review. This is the same project shown in Figure 2–1.

Figure 1–3 shows a very simple PERT network, and is really nothing more than what was done using the backwards planning method. As was the case with the backwards planning method, the PERT technique shows that preparing for the management presentation will take about five working days, and that means work should start immediately. The PERT network offers another key advantage, however. It visually depicts the logical flow of tasks. This makes it easier to see if any tasks have been left out. It also makes it easier to determine if any tasks can be worked in parallel (thereby reducing the total time required for the project).

Suppose, for example, that a room and a projector are reserved at the start of the effort, and the rehearsals are conducted with the rough draft of the presentation charts (instead of waiting for the completed artwork). The PERT network for this alternate process is shown in Figure 1–4. Note that this approach allows cutting a full day off the time required to prepare for the project. That time could be used to do something else.

Figure 1–4 also shows the critical path concept. The critical path is the one that requires the most time to complete, and therefore determines the project minimum completion time. Other paths through the

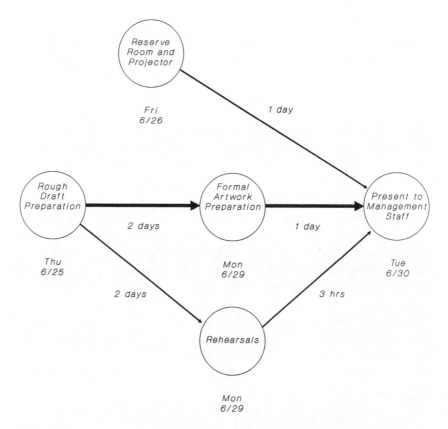

Figure 1–4. A modification of the plan shown in Figures 2 and 3. This PERT network shows that total preparation time can be reduced from five to four days (if rehearsals are done from a rough draft, and a room and a printer are requested while other tasks are being worked). Note that the critical path takes longest, and is shown with heavy arrows.

PERT network require less time. The critical path is shown with a heavy arrow. In Figure 1–4 this is the center path, which consists of rough draft preparation, artwork preparation, and the presentation. This path is the critical path because it requires three days, which is longer than other paths through the PERT network.

The example can be taken one step further. Suppose your boss changes his request. Instead of asking you to give a presentation on only one of your projects, your boss now wants each of the four people who report to you to give presentations at the same meeting. Figure 1–5 shows the PERT network for this project, and it illustrates several interesting points. One thing to note is that all four sets of rough drafts will arrive at the art department simultaneously. This should alert you to check with the art department to see if they can handle all four presentations in one day. Suppose you do this, and the people in the art department tell you the work will take three days. After adding this to the PERT network in Figure 1–5, it becomes apparent that the total preparation time is now seven days. Unless you make some changes, your group won't be ready to give the presentations next Tuesday.

At this point, it becomes necessary to rearrange the events to shorten the total required preparation time so that your group will be ready for next Tuesday's meeting. Figure 1–6 is a further revision of the PERT network shown in Figure 1–5. It shows how your group can be ready for the Tuesday meeting by rehearsing with rough drafts while the art department prepares the formal presentation materials. Note that in this plan, the rehearsals are initiated as soon as the rough drafts are available. The rehearsals will be conducted on Thursday and Friday, instead of waiting until the following Monday, which allows time to make modifications if the rehearsals show a need for change. In Figure 1–6, the critical path is preparing the rough drafts and the formal artwork. By working the rehearsals in parallel, though, the presentations can be ready for the Tuesday deadline. The PERT network in Figure 1–6 also shows that the logical inter-relationships of all the events still make sense; in other words, the completion of each event allows progressing to the next.

GANTT CHARTS

Gantt charts show the time-phasing and scheduling of events necessary to reach an objective. A bar chart format is used. To illustrate the concept, consider the first example in this chapter—preparing a project review for presentation in one week. Figure 1–7 shows a Gantt chart for the schedule of events to complete the assignment.

There are several problems that limit the effectiveness of Gantt charts as planning tools, though. One of the most immediate is defining a series of events that will ultimately result in accomplishment of the objective. *There's nothing inherent to the Gantt chart development process that assures the completion of one task will logically allow initiation of the next, or that all necessary tasks have been identified.* For that reason, a Gantt chart alone is a poor management review tool, even though they are widely used for that purpose.

Gantt charts are best used as a management aid *after* a plan has been developed with the backwards planning or PERT method. Once either the backwards planning or the PERT method has identified all necessary tasks, these tasks can be shown on a Gantt chart; then the Gantt

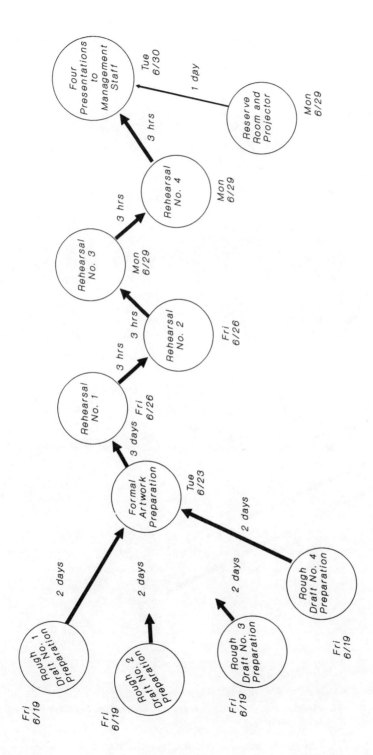

Figure 1–5. A PERT network for four presentations, all to be given on the same day. Notice the heavy load placed on the art department, when all four rough drafts arrive simultaneously.

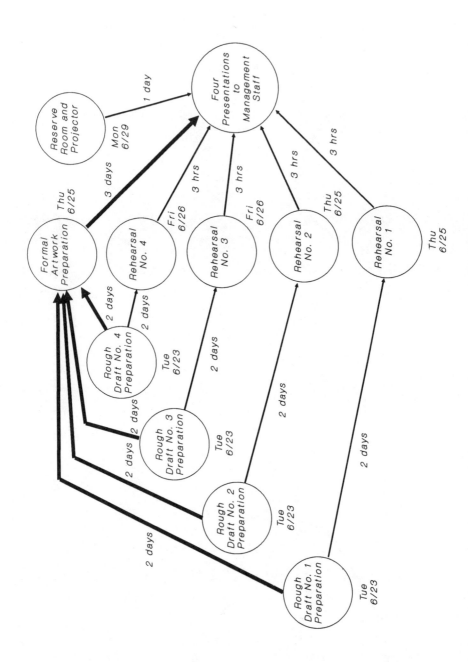

Figure 1–6. A modification of the plan presented in Figure 1–5. The modification allows shortening the presentation time to five days, thereby meeting the required completion date.

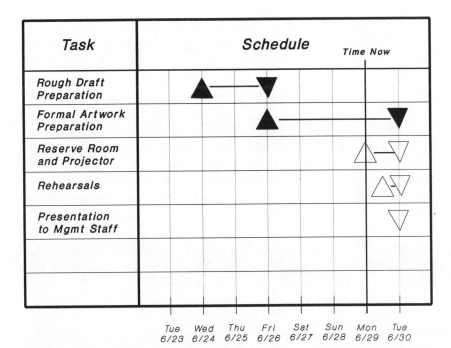

| Task | Schedule | | | | | Time Now | | |

Tue 6/23 Wed 6/24 Thu 6/25 Fri 6/26 Sat 6/27 Sun 6/28 Mon 6/29 Tue 6/30

Figure 1–7. A Gantt chart for the first example presented in this chapter.
Triangles indicate milestones. Initiation of a task is represented by an
upward-pointing triangle, an inverted triangle represents completion of a
task, and filling in a triangle indicates the milestone was met. The "time
now" line is used to track progress. If today is Monday, the chart shows
that rough draft and formal artwork preparation are complete, but reserv-
ing a room and projector has not yet been initiated.

chart can be used to track progress. This is accomplished by moving a
vertical line to represent "time now." All tasks to the left of the "time
now" line should be complete; if they are not, they are behind schedule. This concept is further illustrated in Figure 1–7.

CONCLUSIONS

This chapter discussed the importance of planning. Backwards planning, the PERT method, and Gantt charts were covered. These are
useful planning techniques, and they can help to avoid a common
management problem. A frequently voiced complaint of senior executives is that when subordinates fail to meet commitments, it's invaria-
bly due to poor planning.

Planning takes practice and mental discipline to define your organization's objectives, and then to create a logical sequence of events that will allow meeting those objectives. Simply jumping into the job and doing something might seem easier, but in the long run, it's not. Our observations and experience show that this approach frequently leads to disaster.

One final need is for flexibility. A plan should describe those tasks that will logically allow accomplishment of an objective. Frequently one finds that during the execution of a plan, knowledge or circumstances change, and this change may indicate a need to modify the plan. Don't hesitate to do that. We've seen situations in which obviously obsolete plans were doggedly followed, with predictably poor results.

Planning (and its results) are very visible management skills. As a manager, you are responsible for achieving results by directing the work of others. Proper planning is absolutely essential to do this effectively.

Further Reading

Rosenau, Milton D., *Successful Project Management*, Wadsworth, Inc., 1981.

Cummings, Thomas G., and Srivastva, Suresh, *Management of Work*, University Associates, 1977.

Caplow, Theodore, *How to Run Any Organization*, The Dryden Press, 1976.

Hays, Col. Samuel H., and Thomas, Ltc. William N., *Taking Command*, Stackpole, 1967.

Murdick, Robert G., and Ross, Joel E., *Information Systems for Modern Management*, Prentice-Hall, Inc., 1975.

Halsey, William, D., *Macmillan Contemporary Dictionary*, Macmillan Publishing Company, Inc., 1979.

Chapter 2
BUDGETING

Management, in its simplest definition, consists of two functions—planning and controlling. The previous chapter discussed planning, and presented methodologies for identifying all of the tasks necessary to reach an objective. Controlling is a logical continuation of the management process. It consists of two activities—budgeting, and tracking costs against the budget. This chapter discusses budgeting.

Budgeting is the process of assigning costs to the tasks identified in the planning process, and developing estimates for the cost of the total project. Simply stated, a budget is an estimate of what it will cost to implement a planned course of action. Business organizations prepare many different kinds of budgets, but the basic budget from which all budgets in a company flow is the master budget. The master budget, which is usually prepared by the company's chief financial officer, defines overall business objectives. Since the objective of a business is to make a profit, these objectives are expressed in monetary terms. Other budgets are prepared to support the master budget. These typically include the sales budget, the procurement budget, the manufacturing budget, the personnel budget, the overhead budget, and others. Budgets are prepared at all management levels in an organization (from first-level managers to chief executive officers). Budgets may be prepared for specified reporting periods, such as annual or quarterly budgets, or to identify costs for a particular project.

Budgets are prepared for two reasons. Budgets identify the resources required to run a business, or to complete a project. Budgets also provide a means for comparing actual expenses to planned expenses, thereby providing a means for evaluating performance.

In this book, the emphasis will be on budgeting skills required for first-level managers. That means the emphasis will be on the budgeting skills necessary to develop project costs, and for managing the efforts of a small work group.

THE BUDGETING PROCESS

As a first-level manager, you will almost certainly be required to prepare budgets. At the first level of management, these budgets usually focus on specific projects and the annual operating expenses of the group. Projects are activities and tasks that have defined starting and stopping points, with the stopping point usually being the completion of the project. Annual operating expenses are generally non-profit specific, such as advertising, displays, office supplies, sick leave, etc.

In some cases, depending on the nature of the organization, first-level managers may be required to prepare one or more of the major budgets mentioned earlier. For example, the manager of the accounting department may be required to prepare the cash flow budget, or the manager of the sales department may be required to prepare the sales budget. Specialized budgets of this type are beyond the scope of this chapter and will not be dealt with here.

BUDGETING APPROACHES

Budget estimates can be expressed in man-hours or dollars. In larger companies, for example, first-level managers frequently express their budgets in terms of man-hours required to complete a project, or man-hours allocated for training, vacation, sick leave, etc. In these companies, the man-hour estimates will then be converted to dollars by the accounting department. In smaller companies, first-level managers will probably be required to do both in order to arrive at a dollar estimate.

Whether budgets are estimated in dollars, man-hours, or some combination of the two, a method is needed for developing the estimates. There have traditionally been two approaches to this problem. The first is the top-down method, in which upper management states what the budget will be (either directly, or through a separate estimating department). In the top-down approach, the people doing the work simply accept the budget, and work to meet it. Our experience, however, shows that there are serious disadvantages to this approach. Because the people doing the work have no say in preparing the budget, top-down budgeting tends to be demotivating. And because the people doing the estimating are not the people who do the work, the budgets are more likely to be either too high or too low. Either situation is bad.

Many business organizations today use the bottom-up approach, in which the people doing the work (or buying the supplies or services) estimate the budget. We favor this approach, because our experience shows that budgets tend to be more realistic when the people closest to

Chipotle

BURRITOS & TACOS
WWW.CHIPOTLE.COM

Guacamole-colored Guacamole.

610 W. Diversey
773-281-1492

t: maria   04/10/2006
ER #340   5:51 PM
                                       10241

bacoa   5.75

Total   5.75
                                         0.59

Total   6.34
                                        20.04
                                        13.70

--- Check Closed ---

the work prepare the estimates. The bottom-up budgeting approach also tends to instill a sense of ownership, which helps to make the budget more acceptable to those affected by it.

BUDGETING PITFALLS

We have observed several budgeting errors common to new managers. One of these errors is inflated estimates. We believe these are usually the result of insecurity or inexperience. Inexperience can cause inflated estimates simply because the person preparing the estimate does not have the experience base on which to estimate the cost of the project. If you find yourself in this situation, we recommend that prior to finalizing your estimates, you seek the advice of members of your group, your boss, or other first-level managers with similar responsibilities. Their insights can help you to refine your budgets.

Many new managers feel threatened when preparing budgets, especially when they consider that the budget will become one of the primary standards by which their performance will be evaluated. Insecurity can create fears about overrunning budgets, and this can instill a need to throw in a cushion to cover any contingencies. Such contingency funds are often charitably referred to as "management reserves." Placing management reserves in the budget may be acceptable under certain conditions, but the reserve should always be labelled as such. In other words, don't pad other parts of the budget to create a reserve. The reason for this is that concealed management reserves can creep into budgets at every level in the organization, and this can rapidly make an organization noncompetitive. Clear identification of all management reserves allows upper management to budget an appropriate reserve for the entire project.

A good way to identify and prevent inflated estimates is to break the project into smaller subtasks. This better reveals what the project will really consist of, and it is usually easier to accurately estimate the cost of these smaller work elements. Note, however, that this is really nothing more than planning at a more detailed level. Our experience shows that this procedure, along with more detailed planning, frequently results in lower and more accurate estimates.

In some organizations, the estimating process goes all the way down to the people actually doing the work. In this situation, first-level managers are required to review estimates prepared by their direct reports. The process of breaking projects into smaller elements to assess the accuracy of the estimate is particularly useful when subordinates prepare estimates that seem high. The process usually convinces subordinates that budgets can be reduced, and helps to develop their planning skills.

If breaking a project into smaller elements shows that an estimate is too high and a subordinate is unwilling to commit to the project at a lower cost, we recommend that you ask the subordinate to explain why he or she feels more resources are required. Let the subordinate present his or her views, and listen to the explanation. If the reasons are sound, re-evaluate your position. If the reasons do not make sense, though, the best course of action is to assign the subordinate those discrete subtasks for which you have reached cost agreement, and place overall authority for task completion elsewhere. You may wish to keep this authority, or you may decide to assign it to another subordinate.

Occasionally just the opposite situation occurs, and budget estimates seem too low. This can also result from inexperience, as well as a tendency to overcommit. Inexperience can create low estimates for the same reasons it creates high estimates: The person preparing the budget simply does not know what the job will really cost. The approach to guard against this is the same as explained above. Seek help from those with more knowledge.

Our experience shows that the tendency to overcommit is prevalent in new managers. This probably results from a combination of inexperience and a desire to please. Managers at all levels have to be alert to this potential problem. We believe most managers feel they are usually faced with budget requests that seem too high, and by comparison, a low estimate is easy to accept. The problems caused by a low estimate, though, are at least as severe as those caused by inflated estimates. If pricing is based on a project budget that is too low, profit margins will be reduced, and may even disappear. If nonproject budgets are too low (such as the training budget, the entertainment budget, or the overhead budget), your organization probably will not be able to achieve all of its objectives.

BUDGET ESTIMATING STANDARDS

A standard is a measure of comparison used to help formulate an estimate. There are three approaches to using standards to prepare budgets. These are the historical approach, the task-based approach, and the combined historical/task-based approach.

The historical approach bases the estimate on the cost of similar past projects. If your group performs functions that are essentially repeated for new business projects, this approach can work well and be quite accurate. Other factors, however, can destroy the accuracy of estimates based on historical standards. Task dissimilarities or differential worker-experience bases, for example, can quickly cause significant cost changes.

The task-based approach is another estimating method. The idea here is to take a detailed plan, break the major tasks into sub-tasks, estimate each sub-task, and then add the costs to calculate the total. This approach may be the only way to estimate a project that is completely new, that is, unlike any other project ever attempted by your company.

Projects that are completely new won't usually be the case, though, and that allows the use of a third estimating method. This method combines both the historical and the task-based forecasting approaches. Each approach is used to estimate the budget, and then the two are compared. If there are large cost differences, more analysis is required. Even when the cost differences are small, it's a good idea to compare the new project to previous ones to identify any areas that might increase costs or allow savings. A good way to do this is with the risk management tools that will be explained in Chapter 19.

CONCLUSIONS

Budgeting is really little more than developing and assigning costs to the tasks identified during the planning process. This chapter presented several of the subtleties associated with budgeting, and discussed ways to increase the accuracy of this process. Developing accurate budgets is important. If budgets are too high, customers will go to competitors. If budgets are too low, profits will shrink, and your company may even lose money. When this happens, schedules and quality suffer, and customers will again be driven to competitors.

On a more personal level, remember that one of the main reasons budgets exist is to provide a standard for evaluating performance. For your personal success, it's important that your budget estimates be realistic, and that your organization adhere to them.

References

Kyle, William W., and Larson, Kermit D., *Fundamental Accounting Principles*, Richard D. Irwin, Inc., 1981.

Kotler, Philip, *Marketing Management*, Prentice-Hall, Inc., 1980.

"Internal Operating Controls," *The Technique of Management*, Aerojet General Corporation pamphlet, 1986.

Francis, Philip H., *Principles of R&D Management*, American Management Associations, 1977.

Chapter 3
TRACKING COSTS

Sally Johnson felt confident about the call from her boss to come to his office. Her group had just completed a major redesign of the company's advertising brochure, and the results were very good. Things had gotten a little hectic near the end of the project, but Sally had assigned additional personnel to the job, and it was completed on time. Sally was proud of the finished brochure. She had carefully planned the work and meticulously prepared the budget. The president of the company had complimented her on the appearance of the new brochure.

Sally knocked on her boss's door, and when he looked up, she walked into the room expecting a compliment. What she received was quite a bit different.

"Sally," her boss began. "Did you know you overran your budget by more than $10,000 on the brochure project?"

Sally was dumbfounded. "I don't understand. . . ." she began.

"Obviously," her boss said.

Sally tried to think about what could have gone wrong. She had reviewed the accounting reports every other week, as soon as they came out. All had shown the project to be on schedule, and within the planned budget. There must be an error, she thought. Her boss must be wrong.

"I checked the accounting tab runs as soon as they came out," Sally said. "Perhaps you have incorrect information."

"No, I don't think so," her boss said. "I've had it checked. According to the final accounting report, you put two extra people on at the end of the project. You were already overrun when you did that, and the extra people you assigned just worsened the problem. Didn't you know where you were on this project?"

***

The preceding two chapters discussed techniques for effective planning and budgeting. Both of these are key management skills. As can be seen from the above example, however, a third skill is required to effectively manage plans and budgets, and that's the ability to track costs effectively. After all, the best plans and most skillfully prepared budgets are of little value if managers fail to track costs to determine where they stand with respect to the plan.

Many managers don't track their own costs, and rely entirely on the accounting department to provide information on expenditures (we have found this to be particularly pronounced in larger companies). This approach is wrong, and many managers' careers have been ruined because they failed to track costs in an effective manner.

Avoiding surprises is the key idea behind tracking costs, and surprises come in many forms. A manager who fails to stay on top of his or her department's expenditures will sooner or later be confronted with a budget overrun. In many companies, being surprised by a significant budget overrun is cause for demotion, reassignment, or even termination. Underrunning a budget can be just as serious, even though many managers (and in particular, new managers) think they are saving the company money. Underruns adversely affect the company's income tax strategy, billing plans, cash requirements, and credibility. Credibility is affected because when you submit estimates for future projects, the customer may think costs are inflated. Underruns are also serious because they usually indicate the project is behind schedule.

There's yet another category of surprises to consider. Many new (and some not so new) managers are surprised near project completion dates to learn that even though costs were incurred at about the planned rate, the project will require much more funding to complete. This is often caused by poor planning or ineffective risk management, but it can also be caused by poor cost tracking. The reason is that costs can be incurred at the predicted rate, but if the tasks that are supposed to be accomplished as the costs are incurred are not completed, additional budget will be required to complete the job.

COST TRACKING TECHNIQUES

The last chapter discussed budgets for different types of expenditures, including project costs and overhead costs, but there are also many other categories of cost. For tracking purposes, almost all cost types can be categorized as having either costs with constant expenditure rates, or costs with nonconstant expenditure rates.

Tracking Constant Expenditure Rates

Many expenditures are incurred at a fairly steady rate. A good example is an overhead budget for office supplies. Suppose your department has been allotted $1,200 for the year, and this budget covers expenditures for such things as pencils, paper, printer ribbons, and other similar items. While it's not likely the expenses for each month will be exactly equal (you'll probably buy more supplies in certain months, and less in others), it's a pretty fair bet the expenditures will be approximately equal from month to month. Since you have $1,200 for the year, you can assume the monthly expenditure rate will be $100, and you can use this figure as a standard for tracking your costs. If you spend $200 in one month, you should recognize that this is significantly above the planned expenditure rate, and you may have a problem. If the deviation from the monthly average is large enough to cause concern, something needs to be done about it. The idea behind tracking these costs is to recognize any problems early, and take appropriate corrective action before things get out of control.

This same concept can be applied to other efforts with constant (or nearly constant) planned expenditure rates. Other overhead budgets usually lend themselves to this kind of cost tracking (for example, maintenance costs, vacation costs, and others). Sometimes projects can be tracked this way, too, if the projects are manloaded. Manloading means that the budget estimate was based on a specified number of people working at a constant rate, instead of being based on the time or money needed for each task. Rental fees for mid- to long-term expenditures are another good example of costs that can be tracked this way.

The method we prefer for tracking overhead budgets is to combine all of the overhead budgets, and track the total on a percentage basis. All of the overhead accounts (maintenance, office supplies, etc.) are combined, and cumulative monthly expenditures are converted to a percentage of the total. We recommend treating overhead man-hour budgets the same way.

This concept can be illustrated with an example. Suppose you are at the end of the third month in the fiscal year. In terms of calendar time, you are at the 25 percent point (three months have gone by, out of a total of twelve months). For the sake of this example, suppose you have spent 26 percent of the overhead dollars, and 23 percent of the overhead man-hours. Comparing the percent of the budget expended to the percent of elapsed calendar time shows a slight dollar budget overrun, and a slight man-hour budget underrun. These trends should be watched, but in this case, the differences between planned and actual expenditures are small enough to be of little concern. If, however, you had only spent 5 percent of the man-hour budget, or 40 percent of the dollar budget, steps should be taken to correct the problem. These steps might consist of restricting overhead dollar expenditures, attempting to convert the overhead man-hours to dollars (which the accounting department may be able to do), or any of several other appropriate management responses.

In the companies we've worked for, a 5 percent variance is usually the threshold allowed before corrective actions are required. This represents a good starting point, but you have to tailor this to the situation. There may be situations in which you feel comfortable with a much larger variance. For example, if the start of a project is delayed by upper management, you can expect a significant cost underrun against the original budget. In such a situation, it's likely that no corrective action would be necessary. Caution and prudence are required when assessing variances from the budget, however. It's very easy to convince yourself that a problem doesn't exist. If you see a variance developing, you have to objectively decide if it is significant, and if any corrective actions are required. The key idea is to find the problem as soon as possible to obtain as much time as you can to correct it.

Tracking Nonconstant Expenditure Rates

Constant expenditure rates are fairly easy to track. However, many budgets include expenditures that occur at a nonconstant rate. Many project budgets, for example, are linked to the completion of discrete subtasks. Such budgets have nonconstant expenditure rates.

Conceptually, this problem is only slightly more complex than that of tracking constant expenditure rates. For constant expenditure rates, the outflow of resources should occur at a rate that essentially remains unchanged. Tracking nonconstant expenditures requires identifying what the actual costs for each task are, when these costs occur, and then comparing what is being spent to what should be spent.

Another example will be used to illustrate this concept. Suppose you are managing a project that consists of seven major subtasks, as shown in the Figure 1 PERT network. Let's further suppose you prepared a budget for these tasks in accordance with the guidance provided in Chapter 2. In this budget, you estimated the cost for each task in man-hours, as follows.

Task	Budget
A	40 hours
B	40 hours
C	70 hours
D	150 hours
E	30 hours
F	140 hours
G	70 hours

The information in the above table and the PERT network of Figure 1 show what the expenditures should be, and when they should occur. You now need a good management tool to provide visibility into how well the actual expenditures compare to the planned expenditures, and whether any unacceptable trends are developing.

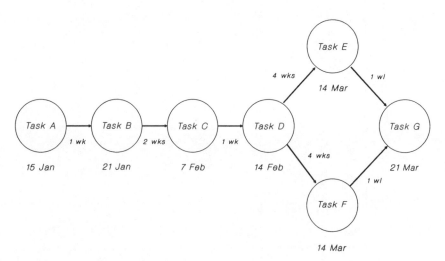

Figure 3–1. PERT network for an example project. The milestone chart and time-phased spend plan for this project are shown in Figure 3–2.

Milestone charts with time-phased spend plans fill this need. Such a chart is shown in Figure 3–2, which shows the milestones (and their time phasing) for the PERT network of Figure 3–1. Note that each task is represented by a triangle, and is shown at the point in time it should occur. Time is measured along the X-axis. The cumulative costs are shown along the Y-axis. Planned expenditures are generally shown by a solid line connecting the milestones.

If a milestone occurs on schedule and the cumulative expenditures equal the planned expenditures, the triangle for the original milestone is darkened to signify completion. If the milestone occurs earlier or later than planned, or cumulative costs exceed or underrun planned costs, a new milestone is drawn in and darkened upon completion. The original milestone remains on the chart, however, to illustrate deviations from the plan. An arrow is usually drawn from the original milestone to the new one, to clearly show deviations from the plan. Dotted lines are drawn between the darkened milestones to show actual expenditures.

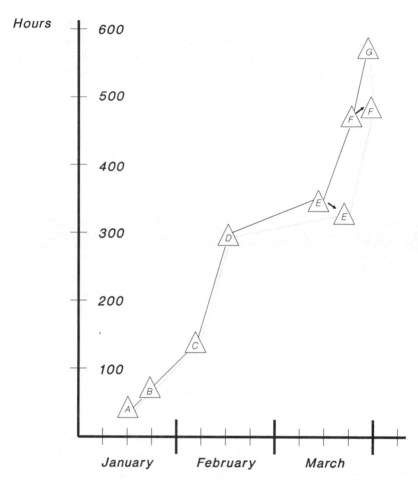

Figure 3–2. A milestone chart with time-phased spend plan. The solid line represents planned expenditures; the dotted line represents actual expenditures. Note that the project is proceeding on schedule until Task E, at which time the actual expenditure rate falls off. The project manager recognized this problem, and increased the expenditure rate to bring the project back on schedule.

Dotted lines are drawn in Figure 3–2 to represent actual expenditures. Note that everything is on schedule and on budget up to Task D. After Task D, however, the expenditure rate falls off, and the project starts to fall behind schedule. As can be seen from the direction of the dotted lines after Task D, the person managing the project recognized the problem, and assigned additional manpower. This is shown by the sharp increase in expenditures occurring after the second week in

March, which brings the project back on schedule. As was the case for tracking constant expenditure rates, the idea behind the milestone chart and its associated time-phased spend plan is to provide the visibility needed to recognize deviations as soon as possible, and allow time to take appropriate corrective action.

PITFALLS

As can be seen from the above examples, the philosophy behind tracking costs is rather straightforward. The primary purpose of cost tracking is to prevent surprises, and the techniques presented here allow one to do this. There are a few pitfalls to watch out for, however. These are described below.

Accounting Reports

The beginning of this chapter mentioned the fallacy inherent in relying on accounting reports to track an organization's costs. This problem seems particularly prevalent in new managers. The problem with relying on accounting reports is not one of accuracy—it's one of timeliness.

Most companies' accounting reports are at least two to three weeks old by the time the manager sees them (our experience shows that in many cases this figure is closer to six weeks). Simply stated, managers can't afford to rely on information this old. In order to properly manage expenditures, one needs to know about them either before they occur or as they occur. In order to do this, we recommend developing a system within your group to provide this visibility.

You may wish to keep track of expenditures yourself, and for new managers, this is probably a good idea (at least initially, in order to become familiar with your group's financial affairs). If your group is large enough, hiring a full-time financial administrator may be prudent. For most first-level managers, though, this is usually not possible. You may be able to get around this problem by requiring each of your subordinates to track their own costs, with you reviewing them on a regular basis. Another option is to delegate this task to a selected subordinate as an additional duty. This approach can be advantageous to both the manager and the assigned subordinate. (It helps to develop the subordinate, while simultaneously giving the manager more time to concentrate on other management responsibilities.) If you are able to use this approach, be careful not to ignore your group's financial situation. You may be able to delegate some of the work in tracking the costs, but you are still responsible for your group's performance.

Dynamic Situations

Everything discussed so far assumed that planned work and expenditures are proceeding approximately on schedule. In well-managed organizations, this is usually the case. There will be situations, however, that require a higher-than-planned expenditure rate (perhaps in a crisis situation, or when a rapid solution to a complex problem is needed). These are the situations you really have to watch out for, especially on small projects. If you run into a problem on a small project (e.g., one with a total budget of only a few hundred hours), you could easily exceed the total budget in a very short period of time by assigning extra people. In dynamic situations, extra attention to cost tracking is a necessity.

Working Without Budget

In most companies, managers are issued funding to meet project requirements. This funding is, in effect, the budget to do the job. Unfortunately, it's easy to let budget discipline lapse, particularly if you or your group are willing to do extra work without additional budget. The usual result is an overrun, with you (as the manager) being held accountable. This is a tough spot to be in.

Good planning, budgeting, and cost tracking techniques help to avoid this problem by clearly defining the tasks your group is funded to accomplish. Our experience shows that this is an area where one has to stand firm. If you are asked to do an out-of-scope task (in other words, one that is not in the plan), you need extra budget. It's tempting to be a hero and take on unfunded work, but it seldom works out well. Never forget that you, not the person who should have provided the extra budget, are responsible for your group's performance. If there's one thing experience has taught us, it's that when you overrun a budget, very few people are willing to share the blame. They will simply (and properly) want to know how you intend to fix the problem.

CONCLUSIONS

In this chapter, three important management concepts were tied together—planning, budgeting, and tracking costs. All of these are critically important management functions, and form the building blocks of basic management skills. As a manager, you're the person who has to make things happen, on schedule, on budget, and in a manner that will achieve planned objectives. Planning and controlling are key to any manager's ability to do this, so it's important that these skills be mastered.

We believe, as do most other management authors, that planning and controlling are the two key elements of management, and that all other management skills are really aimed at refining the process of planning and controlling. Keep this in mind as you read the following sections of this book.

Further Reading

Canada, John R., *Intermediate Economic Analysis for Management and Engineering*, Prentice-Hall, Inc., 1971.

Murdick, Robert G., and Ross, Joel E., *Information Systems for Modern Management*, Prentice-Hall, 1975.

Hays, Colonel Samuel H., *Taking Command*, Stackpole Books, 1967.

Part II
STAFFING AND SUPERVISING

Chapter 4
INTERVIEWING

One of the most challenging tasks faced by any manager is interviewing and selecting new employees. Most people picture a nervous candidate sitting in front of an imposing manager, but the truth is that more often than not, the experience is a trying one for both the interviewer and the person being interviewed. The usual result is that after an hour or two of uncomfortable conversation, the interview is concluded and the manager has insufficient information on which to base a good hiring decision.

The interview should be an opportunity for both the manager and the candidate to get to know each other. Most interviews are necessarily limited in time, so extracting maximum information with a minimum of questions is important. *Questions should encourage the candidate to speak freely, with little prompting by the interviewer.* This both conserves time and gives the interviewer an opportunity to evaluate the candidate's spoken communications skills.

Most managers are fairly adept at identifying a candidate's technical qualifications. The breakdown usually occurs when the manager wants to know more about the candidate as a person. These include such things as the candidate's motivations, problem-solving skills, and the ability to get along with others.

To augment the position-related technical questions that each manager will know best, we suggest six additional questions. These will reveal a great deal about the candidate's personal values, help the interview flow smoothly, and provide an opportunity to evaluate the candidate's ability to think and communicate clearly. Let's examine each, along with interpretations of likely responses.

Question 1. Why are you thinking about leaving your present job?
A good response to this question is a positive one, such as "I feel I can make a larger contribution than my present job allows" or "I feel I am ready for more responsibility." If you get this kind of answer, encourage the candidate to explain why the need for increased responsibility cannot be satisfied in his or her present position. You will learn much about the candidate's self-perception, ability to work with others, strengths, interests, and future goals.

Poor responses to this question are "I want more money" or "I hate my boss." People wanting to change jobs just for more money are naive for revealing such an answer to a prospective employer, and they are unlikely to be loyal, long-term contributors to your organization. Candidates who "hate the boss" suffer from both of the above deficiencies, and probably do not work well with others.

Question 2. What are your strengths?

Most candidates are well-prepared for this question. A proper response should be concise and relate to the position you are trying to fill. A candidate applying for a sales position, for example, might claim to be strong at establishing and maintaining good personal relationships.

If a candidate asserts as a primary strength something totally unrelated to the requirements of the job, though, you will have strong evidence of poor thinking patterns or an inability to recognize key issues. We know of a case, for example, in which a candidate applying for an engineering position described tennis as his greatest strength.

A candidate who takes a long time to develop an answer to this question (or worse yet, cannot offer any strengths) would probably be a poor addition to your staff. Such individuals usually have a very low self-image, and are unable to make decisions.

Question 3. What are your weaknesses?

This can be a most revealing question. A good answer is one that turns a strength into a perceived weakness, such as "I tend to push myself (or my people) too hard" or "I am a fanatic about accuracy." These kinds of answers show the candidate to be meticulous and thorough, yet aware of and sensitive to the limitations of others. Another good response to this question would be the candidate's describing a past mistake, and elaborating upon what was done wrong. This response shows the capability for objective self-evaluation, a willingness to change, and a desire for improvement.

Sometimes the poor answers to this question are almost comical, such as "I tend to be dishonest at times" or "I can't write very well." While such answers are at least honest (and perhaps self-contradicting in the first example), they can reveal traits that might be cause for eliminating the candidate. Another poor answer is "I don't have any weaknesses." Obviously, such a person, at best, lacks the capability for objective self-assessment.

Question 4. Can you tell me about the best manager you ever worked for?

A good response to this question is evident if the candidate describes a favorite manager as a person that "encouraged me to manage my own activities." A strong candidate will probably tell you about a manager who outlined broad goals and then relied on the candidate to determine the appropriate course of action. This shows that the candidate was highly thought of by that employer. It also shows that the candidate welcomes responsibility and requires minimal supervision.

Poor answers to this question include "I liked Manager X because he didn't care when I came in late" or "Manager Y was good because she always told me exactly what to do." Such answers reveal candidates who probably require extra supervision, or who have poor work habits.

Question 5. Can you tell me about the worst manager you ever had?

For reasons similar to those discussed above, a positive answer is one that indicates a disdain for being over-managed. Individuals who do not like excessive supervision are generally self-motivated. A slow response or being unable to recall a poor manager is also a good sign. If a candidate is genuinely unable to answer this question, chances are he or she works well with others.

We would recommend not hiring a candidate who replies with "I didn't like Manager Z because she expected me to figure out how to get a job done." This answer shows the candidate needs someone else to do his or her thinking. Other poor (and revealing) answers include "He gave me too much to do" or "She didn't give me a big enough raise."

Question 6. What are the main problems you face at your current job, and how are you solving them?

A good candidate will respond quickly to this question, showing that he or she is continually defining and solving problems. A good gauge of a person's values are the priorities assigned to the problems faced in the current position. If the candidate perceives the main problems to be procedural or technical, he or she can see beyond the personality issues that will be present in any organization. Strong candidates will have definite ideas about how problems should be solved, and will be able to offer solutions that demonstrate clear thinking abilities.

Weak candidates will respond with such answers as "We have no problems in my present company" or they will focus on personality conflicts. These kinds of answers show the candidate is uninterested in defining and solving new problems, or has difficulty working with others.

***

The above questions can provide better insights to the motivations and capabilities of an applicant than the all-too-common "Where do you want to be in five years" line of questioning. As a manager, you have a significant responsibility in bringing new people into your organization. In today's legal environment, it's much easier to hire than fire a poor choice. And, as a moral issue, a disservice is done both to the individual and to the organization if the wrong person is hired. Finally, the ability to select good new employees is an important (and highly visible) skill for any manager to have. For these reasons, you owe it to yourself and your organization to get the most out of every interview, and that's what the above six questions are designed to do.

Further Reading

Vouck, Philip R., "Recruiting, Interviewing, and Hiring: Staying Within the Boundaries," *Personnel Administrator*, May 1987.

Raudsepp, Eugene, "Interviewing Candidates for Staff Openings," *Machine Design*, April 8, 1982.

Freedman, Howard S., *How to Get a Headhunter to Call*, John Wiley and Sons, Inc., 1986.

Posner, Mitchell J., *Executive Essentials*, Avon Books, 1982.

Chapter 5
DELEGATING

Delegating is an integral part of the management process. No manager can succeed without the ability to delegate in an effective manner. As a new manager, you have to make the transition from doing the work to managing it, and in order to do this, you must delegate to your subordinates.

This chapter discusses the importance of delegation, and presents several techniques for developing good delegating habits. It also discusses barriers to effective delegation found in the manager, subordinates, and the situation, and how these barriers can be overcome. Finally, a five-step process for effective delegation is presented.

As a new manager, you may feel uneasy about delegating. That's a normal feeling when one makes the transition from worker to manager. You became a manager because of your outstanding work, and you want to preserve that reputation. This becomes a requirement for excellence you would like to apply to the group you now manage. You want the group to perform as well as you did, particularly now that you are in charge.

When faced with this situation, many new managers attempt to do the work themselves, or they delegate the work but over-manage it, constantly reviewing progress to assure the job is proceeding properly. The results of this approach are predictable. Subordinates become frustrated, and the manager does not have enough time to manage properly. The manager's efforts to attain a high level of group performance cause exactly the opposite to occur. New tasks only aggravate the cycle, and the performance of the group deteriorates further.

It's important to recognize that managers are evaluated by different criteria than the people they supervise. Workers are evaluated on the quality of their individual work. Managers are evaluated on the quality of their group's performance. Understanding this difference is critically important. A manager who attempts to do well by doing all the work himself is doomed to failure. A manager who doesn't delegate, or who delegates poorly, limited the group's output to that which the manager can personally accomplish. A manager with this problem cannot take on new responsibilities or develop others in the group.

There is also a more subtle reason why an inability to delegate effectively limits a manager's upward mobility. Silverman, in *The*

Technical Manager's Survival Book (McGraw-Hill Book Co., 1984) points out that managers who delegate poorly deny themselves opportunities to explore and master new areas. Silverman recommends that managers delegate all tasks with which they are familiar, and focus on those tasks requiring new skills.

BARRIERS TO EFFECTIVE DELEGATION

Barriers to effective delegation are found in three places: the manager; subordinates; and the situation. There are several reasons these barriers exist. A few hints on how to avoid them follow.

Don't Worry About Being Indispensable. If your subordinates do outstanding work, you might feel you are unnecessary. These fears may cause you to try to make yourself indispensable, but this is a dangerous thing to do for two reasons. Making (or attempting to make) yourself indispensable stifles group development. Your people will never get the opportunity to face the challenges needed to develop new skills. And if you succeed in making yourself indispensable, you've probably killed any chances for future advancement. After all, if you're indispensable, how can you be promoted? You'll be too valuable in your current assignment.

Don't Let Crises Become a Habit. Business circumstances may prohibit delegating certain critical tasks. In a crisis situation, for example, your boss may direct you personally to work on a problem. In some cases, depending on urgency, you may decide to do this on your own. You need to be careful about deciding what constitutes a crisis, though. Our observations lead us to believe that everything is a crisis for some managers, and this mentality justifies the manager doing the work (at least in the manager's mind). For these managers, every new assignment is a crisis.

Don't Try to Do It All Yourself. You became a manager by demonstrating superior competence in the skills you now supervise. Attaining that excellence was a key element to your advancement. You may therefore feel it's easier simply to do the work yourself instead of explaining it to someone else. That may be true in the short run, but in the long run it's counterproductive. Doing the work yourself limits the new responsibilities you can accept, and stifles development of your subordinates. If your department is understaffed, you will have to shoulder an increased workload until you hire the people you need. If this situation exists in your department, though, don't allow yourself to become too busy to interview.

Understand the Task You Are Delegating. If you are uncertain or unclear on the tasks to be accomplished, you will be unable to delegate the work in an effective manner. In some cases you may understand the task, but you may not be able to explain it clearly. Or if you are uncertain about what your group is responsible for, your subordinates will be even more confused when they attempt to do the work. It's important to have a clear idea of your group's responsibilities, or you won't be able to effectively delegate the work to your subordinates.

Trust Your Subordinates. There is no doubt you could do certain individual tasks better than your subordinates can. But you are now managing the efforts of a group. You may be a more capable individual, but you cannot outperform the collective efforts of your subordinates. If you never delegate the difficult tasks, your subordinates will never develop their capabilities. In fact, their capabilities will probably deteriorate. It is frustrating to watch your people make mistakes, but those mistakes are essential to their development.

Overcome Subordinate Limitations. A subordinate's inexperience, inability to organize, avoidance of work, or overdependence on you, the manager, can be overcome by carefully structuring and planning tasks. Ways to do this are examined briefly in this chapter, and covered in more detail in the chapters on planning and counselling. Inadequate incentives can also create an unwillingness in some subordinates to accept increased responsibilities. To prevent this from becoming a barrier to delegation, you need to ask yourself if the delegated responsibilities are matched by appropriate grades and salaries. If the answer is no, work with your boss and the personnel department (if your company is large enough to have one) to correct the situation.

FIVE STEPS TO DELEGATING EFFECTIVELY

Now that you understand the necessity for delegation, and the major barriers to it that you must overcome, here is a useful five-step process for delegating. This process is shown in Figure 5–1 and explained below.

IDENTIFY ALL TASKS

As a manager, you are responsible for everything your group does or fails to do. This concept is absolute, and if you want to be successful as a manager, you must accept it. The first critical step in meeting this responsibility is identifying and tracking all of the tasks your group

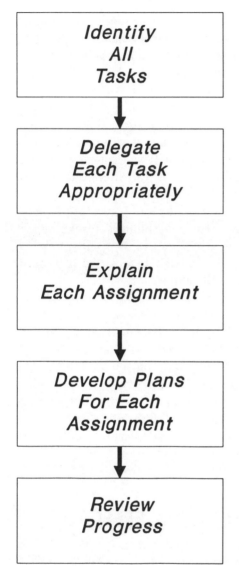

Figure 5–1. *The five-step process of effective delegation.*

must accomplish. There are several ways to do this, but we feel the best is to keep a list.

Successful people are compulsive list-makers, and for good reasons. As your responsibilities increase, you'll simply have too many things going on to be able to rely on your memory alone. We recommend scheduling time on a weekly basis, or more often if necessary, to update this list. If you've never developed a task list for your group, you'll probably be surprised by the number of things it contains. That's good, because it should show you that there are far more activities than you can do yourself.

The format for such a list can be a simple list of things to do, or it can be a more elaborate presentation that describes the problem, the actions required to resolve it, who is responsible for each action, and when these actions must be completed. The latter approach works particularly well in groups with numerous and diverse complex tasks. An example of such a list, taken from the engineering department in an aerospace company, is shown in Figure 5–2. Such lists also form excellent issue tracking systems, and serve to prevent problems from "falling through the cracks."

DELEGATE EACH TASK APPROPRIATELY

The military has a saying about delegation: "Never ask anyone to do anything you wouldn't do yourself." The saying is a good one. The idea behind it is that it would be improper to ask anyone to do a job so distasteful or dangerous you wouldn't do it yourself.

The saying is also true in the business world, but it has a corollary: "Never do anything yourself if you can get somebody else to do it." This thought does not countermand the wisdom of the first saying, nor is it intended to instill an elitist attitude. Rather, its intent is to give you more time to do what you are getting paid for, and that's to manage.

With this in mind, look at the list of tasks you have compiled. Identify the tasks that you should do, and those that can be delegated to your subordinates. The tasks that can be delegated (which probably comprise most of the list) should now be assigned to particular subordinates. To do this, ask yourself what skills each task requires, and who in your group has the best blend of these skills. You may be constrained by the subordinates' areas of job specialization, but that probably won't always be the case. And even if it is, you may want to make the assignment anyway. We've found that what may appear to be constraints imposed by requirements for specialized skills are often opportunities to develop subordinates' abilities in new areas.

EXPLAIN EACH ASSIGNMENT

Understanding and properly communicating assignments is a critical aspect of effective delegation. This means that you have to decide what it is that you want the subordinate to do, and that decision takes some

Issue No.	Description	Required Action	Responsible Engineer	Completion Date
1	Hydraulic tubes leak when system starts.	Define pressure fluctuations during startup transition.	Jones	Complete
		Test individual system components to determine pressure carrying capabilities.	Thompson	18 Feb
		Identify any areas where design is inadequate.	Thompson	22 Feb
2	Quality of change paper (ECPs, etc.) is low. Numerous typographical errors and poor descriptions of requested change makes documents difficult to understand.	Daily 4:00 pm review of all outgoing paperwork.	Hodge	25 Feb
		Review all current paperwork; recall and rewrite as necessary.	Babcock	27 Feb
		Implement tracking system for quality of submitted paperwork.	Allison	28 Feb
3	Proposal submittals are not responsive to customer requirements.	Create compliance cross-index to identify all requirements, and how proposal is responsive to each requirement.	Weinstein	1 Mar

Figure 5–2. One sheet taken from an issue tracking system used to manage numerous complex tasks. This system defines the problems, states what actions are necessary to correct them, assigns the appropriate personnel, and specifies required completion dates.

thought. Deciding what you want the subordinate to accomplish doesn't mean deciding what you want the answer to be, and it may not mean how you want the subordinate to do the job.

For example, suppose you want a subordinate to answer a specific question. Depending on the subordinate's capabilities and experience, it may or may not be necessary for you to describe *how* the answer should be discovered. Perhaps the task is less well-defined, and you want the subordinate to study a family of concerns to decide what the question should be (and then find the answer to it).

This leads to another concept, which is the *degree of initiative* you expect the subordinate to exercise. In one extreme, you might require the subordinate to keep you constantly advised and come to you for all decisions. This might be the case, for example, if you delegate a task to an inexperienced or passive subordinate. At the other end of this spectrum, you may want the subordinate to solve the problem without involving you. The decision should be based on the urgency of the problem and the subordinate's capabilities. Regardless of the approach you select, *make sure the subordinate understands what is expected.*

One of our acquaintances who manages a group of computer programmers failed to adequately explain what he expected a subordinate to do, and this failure lead to a dissatisfied customer. Tom managed a small section of software writers who developed custom software packages. Tom discovered an error in a program that had already been delivered to the customer, and directed a fairly inexperienced programmer *to correct the specific error*. The programmer did this (at the customer's facility), but neglected to run the entire program to verify that it would work with the modification. Unfortunately, it did not, and the new problem was discovered by the customer. The mistake was not the subordinate's. He did exactly what he was told to do. Based on his level of experience, he didn't recognize the need to verify that the program would run properly with the modification. Tom failed to explain to the subordinate the degree of initiative he expected, and the results were predictable.

Another situation involving almost exactly the opposite problem can be shown by an incident that occurred in the Army. The incident involved a newly commissioned lieutenant and an even newer soldier in a basic training company. The lieutenant told the soldier to clean the windows in the soldier's barracks. The soldier happened to be on the third floor. He created quite a ruckus when he carefully climbed through a window and maneuvered along a four-inch sill *outside the barracks* to clean the windows' exterior surfaces. In this case, the person to whom the task had been delegated exercised far too much initiative. Again, the fault lay with the manager (in this case, the lieutenant) who failed to properly explain the assignment.

Finally, when delegating work to subordinates, *explain why the task is necessary.* Most people are better motivated and make better decisions when they understand how their work fits into the big picture. For example, if you ask a secretary to work overtime to finish a report, she'll probably feel better about doing the work if she understands why the overtime is required (perhaps the report is needed to close an important sale). Or suppose you supervise a manufacturing area and ask the people in your department to clean their work area at the end of each shift. Explain that a clean area enhances safety, or that the next shift has a right to enter a clean work area, or simply that senior management has requested better housekeeping. Our experience shows that whatever the reason, subordinates to whom tasks have been delegated generally do a better job if they understand why the tasks are necessary.

DEVELOP A PLAN FOR EACH ASSIGNMENT

Most projects will fail without a plan of action. The plan should define how the task will be approached. It should identify all necessary subtasks and their completion dates.

Depending on the subordinate's experience, the plan may be prepared by you, the subordinate, or the two of you. If you let your subordinates take the lead in developing a plan (and you act as the reviewer or a coach, instead of dictating the plan), they will generally do a better job of adhering to it. (For a more detailed discussion on planning, refer to Chapter 1.)

REVIEW PROGRESS

Even though you delegate tasks, you are still responsible for their outcome. This means you should review progress on a regular basis. The degree of supervision you exercise during these progress reviews (and how often you conduct them) will largely depend on the subordinate's experience. If you review progress too often, your actions will be perceived as inexperience on your part or distrust of the subordinate. Any of these perceptions will probably discourage the subordinate.

To get around this problem, include progress reviews as an integral part of the plan for accomplishing the task. This lets the subordinate know how frequently you plan to review progress, and if he or she feels it's too often, the issue can be resolved during the planning stages.

CONCLUSIONS

Our observations indicate that effective delegation is not usually a natural skill. Delegation is a skill that must be developed, and that takes a dedicated effort on your part. Without good delegating skills, the output of the effort you manage will largely be limited to that which you alone can do. That greatly limits the effectiveness of the group, stifles subordinate motivation, creativity, and development, and ultimately, will limit your survivability as a manager. Good delegating skills, on the other hand, can greatly magnify the output of your group, expand the capabilities of subordinates and your group, and provide tremendous leverage to the direction you want the group to move in.

Further Reading

Silverman, Melvin, *The Technical Manager's Survival Book*, McGraw-Hill Book Company, 1984.

Drucker, Peter F., "Managerial Communications," in *Management—Tasks, Responsibilities, and Practices*, Harper and Row, 1974.

Connelly, J. Campbell, *A Manager's Guide to Speaking and Listening*, American Management Association, 1967.

Hitt, William D., *Management in Action*, Battelle Press, 1985.

Webber, Ross A., *Management: Basic Elements of Managing Organizations*, Richard D. Irwin, Inc., 1979.

Chapter 6
PROMOTIONS

Promotions are one of the most effective motivators available to managers. In fact, the concepts of motivation and promotion are so closely linked they share a common linguistic heritage. Both words evolved from the Latin *motus*, which means to move forward or to set in motion. Promotions can have exactly this effect if they are handled effectively, motivating the person being promoted as well as others in the organization.

This chapter will focus on two issues. The first is promotion selection criteria. This subject is critically important, yet according to Dr. Garda Bowman (former director of the National Conference of Christians and Jews Merit Promotion Project), promotions are frequently based on criteria that are anything but rational. A second important consideration, but one that receives little attention, is maximizing the effectiveness of promotions. When properly administered, promotions can motivate both individuals and groups. When handled poorly, they can be terribly demotivating, even to the person being promoted. This chapter will discuss how to maximize the benefits to be gained from a promotion both at the individual and group level, and how to avoid potentially demotivating aspects of the promotion process.

PROMOTION SELECTION CRITERIA

As a new manager, you probably will not be able to promote individuals to supervisory positions. You probably will, however, have the authority to recommend individuals for promotion to higher-graded, nonsupervisory positions within your group. Before discussing the rationale behind effective promotion decisions and recommendations, a review of the two categories of promotions is in order. These are promotions to positions of increased managerial responsibility, and promotions to higher-graded nonsupervisory positions. Many companies offer both types of career advancement, which provides an avenue of progression (and a source of motivation) for those who do not wish to supervise the work of others.

Increased Managerial Responsibility. This category of promotions involves advancements to positions of greater responsibility. These promotions generally advance the person from a nonsupervisory to a supervisory position, or from a lower to a higher tier supervisory position. Examples include promotions from worker to foreman, salesperson to sales manager, and engineering manager to engineering director.

Advanced Work Content. The second family of promotions involves significant changes in work content, but do not require the person being promoted to assume supervisory responsibilities. Promotions from secretary to administrator, or from inspector to quality assurance engineer, are good examples. Other such promotions are associated with increased seniority in the organization based on a demonstrated increase in the promoted individual's capabilities. Examples include promotions from buyer to senior buyer, senior engineer to engineering specialist, or secretary to senior secretary.

Maintaining a career progression that offers dual avenues of advancement is particularly appealing to large, technically oriented organizations. According to E. X. Hallenberg, a management researcher who studied the effectiveness of this concept at General Electric, the dual career path works well by offering the use of promotions as motivators for individuals who wish to advance in other than managerial roles.

PROMOTION SELECTION CRITERIA

An important first step when considering an individual for promotion (and one that can save both the manager and the candidate for promotion a great deal of time and embarrassment) is to first determine if your company has published guidelines on promotion selection criteria. The best place to get an answer to this question is from your personnel department. Don't be discouraged if you find out no such criteria exists, though. In our experience, that's the case more often than not.

If promotion criteria within your organization has been formalized, the selection process is greatly simplified. If no such criteria exists, you'll have to develop your own. Promotion criteria should include such characteristics as personal integrity, logical thought patterns, good planning skills, and the ability to work well with others (in particular, the ability to interface effectively with subordinates, peers, and superiors).

In addition to the generally applicable characteristics identified above, our experience shows that promotion selection criteria should be tailored to the job. Suppose, for example, that a job opening exists that presents a promotion opportunity. To simplify the example, assume it's for a nonsupervisory position. In order to identify the best candidate for the job, a logical starting point is to first list the job requirements. Be specific, but don't restrict the criteria to the technical job skill requirements. If the job requires interfacing with customers or higher management, for example, candidates will have to be considered in light of that perspective. If the job requires strong writing skills, it would be foolish to consider someone who has shown deficiencies in this area.

Suppose another opening develops outside your group for a first-level supervisory position, and you have been asked to recommend someone or comment on someone being considered for that position. In this case, the candidate should be assessed from two sets of perspectives. The first is a leadership and management perspective, and the second is the technical and interpersonal perspective discussed earlier. Does the person have the ability to plan, coordinate, and lead the activities of others? More significantly (and based on your experience with the potential candidate), would you feel comfortable working with this person?

There's one last issue to consider before recommending someone to a supervisory position, and that's whether the person desires to enter supervision. Not everyone does, and we have found that those who don't usually have strong feelings about it. For reasons to be discussed later, it may not always be wise to directly ask if the individual is interested in entering supervision. Such a question would inform the individual he or she is being considered for promotion. Until the decision has been made, this is a poor practice. If you know your people, though, you should be aware of their career aspirations.

Let's now examine another situation. Suppose you want to promote an individual in your group to a higher level nonsupervisory position (based on a strong track record of above-average performance), but no opening currently exists. Like all promotion recommendations, promotions such as these should also be based on fair and impartial selection criteria. A good way to initiate the selection process is to examine other individuals in the company who are in similar higher-graded positions, and compare their credentials to those held by your candidate. To take an extreme case, if everyone else in the higher classification has a doctorate and your candidate does not, it might be wise to reconsider the recommendation. Other areas of comparison might include years of experience, time in current classification, and level of contribution. In our experience, level of contribution is probably the most significant discriminator. If the candidate is contributing more than others towards work unit goals and objectives, a promotion recommendation is probably warranted (particularly if superior performance has been demonstrated for a sustained period of time).

It is also important to recognize that it would be foolish to exclude someone simply because they do not meet all of the criteria (technical or otherwise) that you have established for a particular job opening. If a candidate has the mental capacity and determination to overcome a lack of specific position-related experience, he or she may well represent the best choice.

One final thought concerns the subject of documentation. If you have a superior performer who is likely to become a candidate for promotion in the future, we strongly recommend documenting the candidate's areas of superior performance. Make your records as specific and quantitative as possible, as good documentation can often make the difference in getting a promotion approved. This is particularly true in larger organizations, where personnel departments will probably be unfamiliar with the individual being considered for promotion, but play a key role in the decision-making process.

MOTIVATIONAL ASPECTS

Managers and organizations frequently make mistakes when administering promotions, which can greatly dampen or destroy the motivational aspects of a promotion (even if the decision to promote is sound). The motivational aspects of promotions will be examined from two perspectives—that of the individual, and that of the group. It's important to recognize that both of the promotion categories discussed earlier (managerial and nonmanagerial promotions) share common attributes that can motivate the individual being promoted, other individuals, and the group.

Individual Motivators

A promotion makes a management statement, one that says the individual's contributions are significantly above average, and that he or she is accordingly more highly valued by the organization. To the individual, a promotion not only represents recognition, prestige, and increased income, but also the payment of a debt. The debt was incurred when the individual performed in an above-average manner over a sustained period of time. In that sense, promotions motivate sustained superior performance, because they indicate the organization will continue to honor its debts. Promotions make a clear statement: if you work hard and smart, you will move ahead. This concept of honoring an obligation to reward superior performance is important. We've all been around organizations that fail to do this. The general feeling we've observed in such environments is one of individuals not stretching themselves too far. If the organization does not recognize higher levels of contribution, many of those driven by a need for achievement (with career advancement being an important measure) simply will not be as motivated.

Group Motivations

A promotion can also be a powerful motivator to others in the organization (that is, people other than the individual being promoted). Many of these motivators are similar to those described for the individual being promoted. These included a feeling that superior performance will be rewarded, and that the company can be trusted.

There are also more subtle motivators that will be felt by the promoted individual's peers. One of these is the unstated premise that the company is willing (and perhaps even prefers) to promote from within. A promote-from-within philosophy will go a long way to encourage dedication to the organization, commitment, and a never-be-satisfied attitude when it comes to workplace efficiency. Our experience shows that most individuals recognize that opportunities continuously develop (due to personnel turnover, retirement, and other promotions). If there is a feeling the organization will first look within when considering eligible candidates, many individuals will strive to attain eligibility. All of these factors encourage superior performance.

For many people, natural feelings of competitiveness also serve as subtle, yet powerful, motivators. When a co-worker advances, a desire to catch up emerges. If the organization transmits a clear message, others will recognize that the best way to move ahead is through sustained superior performance. Those closest to the promoted individual may feel this even more strongly than the others in the organization. This is not only a proximity phenomenon, but the result of those closest to the promoted individual recognizing that management is aware of and impressed by their group's work.

DEMOTIVATIONAL ASPECTS

In order for all of the motivators discussed above to be effective, promotions have to have been based on demonstrated superior performance. If promotions are predominantly based on such factors as age, seniority within the organization, or personal relationships, others will recognize the inherent unfairness. This will usually have a serious negative effect on both individual and group performance (in fact, many companies forbid hiring of relatives for this reason). Frequently, however, even well-deserved promotions are handled so poorly they become demotivating. There are many ways for this to happen. A few of the more common mistakes are described below.

Jumping the Gun

Managers frequently err by informing individuals they have been recommended for a promotion before the promotion is approved. Larger organizations are at a disadvantage here, as they often contain sizeable bureaucratic elements that affect the administration of promotions (including layers of management, the personnel department, the compensation department, and perhaps others). All of these groups are gates that must be passed prior to approval of the promotion, adding delays of several days or perhaps even weeks to the process of administering the promotion. From personal experience, we know that in the mind of an individual being considered for promotion, delays serve only to induce anxiety. The individual may wonder if the organization (or any of the groups mentioned above) feels that he or she is not qualified. Frequently, the individual will not understand why the process takes so long (especially if this is a first promotion).

As the approval process drags on, it's easy for the individual to become frustrated. This can result in decreased productivity and other outcomes even more severe. Suppose, for example, the individual is informed as soon as a recommendation for promotion is made, and then (after the recommendation winds its way through the bureaucracy), it is disapproved. What will you do then? How will you explain the disapproval to the individual? Will the individual remain motivated? Will he or she continue to trust you, and the management of your company?

Before leaving this topic, one other aspect of the "informing too early" tendency should be examined. This is when a manager informs a subordinate that he or she is being considered for promotion. The implication is that the manager has not yet reached a recommendation decision. In this case, the consequences of a delay (or a decision not to proceed with the promotion recommendation) can be even more severe than those described above, especially for the manager. In the example above, the individual will probably be upset with the bureaucracy. In this case, the manager alone will be held accountable.

We strongly believe it's unwise to say anything about pending promotions until the decision to promote has been approved. You may feel tempted to inform the individual as soon as the process is initiated, but for the reasons explained above, it is best to resist this temptation.

Promotion Inequities

In the long run, pay increases that are not commensurate with the promotion will also be demotivating. Our experience shows that at first the promotion will be satisfying enough, and most of the time people will initially overlook raises that do not reflect the increased stature and responsibilities associated with the new assignment. This feeling soon wears off, however, and if the salary increase is too low, dissatisfaction will ultimately result. The same thing occurs when the title or other benefits being offered to the promoted individual are inconsistent with those of others at the same level.

Contrary to what many managers would like to believe, we believe that most individuals are keenly aware of the general salary ranges, titles, and perquisites that go with each level of management or technical expertise. Misrepresenting the truth about such matters will only come back to haunt you. If the personnel organization in your company will not allow the titles, benefits, and salary you feel should go along with a promotion for one of your subordinates, find out why. If the answer is not satisfactory, escalate the problem until it is resolved or you understand the reason for the inequity.

Asking for this information is important for two reasons. If you escalate an inequity to the personnel organization, there's a good chance it will be corrected. Personnel organizations are usually understaffed, and the administrators making salary and grade adjustments are frequently unaware of the inequities they create. The other reason you should ask for information about an apparent inequity is to prepare yourself for the questions that will inevitably come from the individual you are promoting. Chances are quite good that you will be the one doing the explaining. Even if you don't agree with the explanation, your subordinate will recognize that you cared enough to look into the matter.

PRESENTING THE PROMOTION

The manner in which a promotion is presented will never be forgotten. If it is handled poorly, the effects can be devastating. We know of one promotion so poorly handled it resulted in a resignation. After the promotion had been administratively approved, the manager promoted the person in front of his peers (without discussing it first). In an insensitive attempt at humor, the manager remarked that he was "finally able to get old Jack promoted." Everybody had a good laugh, except Jack.

In discussing the incident with Jack several years later, we noticed that he talked about the event as if it had occurred yesterday. Jack felt belittled by the way the promotion was handled, and in particular, by his former manager's remarks. "I did excellent work at that company," he said, "and I deserved the promotion. I resented the implication that I 'finally' managed to advance, and that my former supervisor had to go to extraordinary lengths to make it happen." Jack told us that he made a decision to resign in the same meeting at which the promotion was announced, and did so as soon as he found a comparable position at another company a short while later.

Jack's experience illustrates several of the more common mistakes that managers can make to turn a promotion into a demotivating experience. A promotion is a serious and solemn event, and must be treated accordingly. When you present the promotion, tell the person why he or she is being promoted. The reasons are probably obvious to you, but they may not be so obvious to the individual. By explaining the reasons for the promotion, you will not only be telling the person that you recognize his or her superior performance, you will also be reinforcing that person's more desirable attributes.

The last lesson to be learned from the above story concerns public promotions. In all cases, we recommend the individual first be offered the promotion privately. If you want to promote the person publicly, you should ask his or her permission after he or she has decided to accept the promotion. This can save both you and the person being promoted a great deal of embarrassment if the promotion is not accepted. A public promotion can also go a long way towards increasing the motivation of both the individual and his or her peers, but only if it is well handled. This means no surprises, and no attempts at humor where the promoted individual's accomplishments are concerned.

In accordance with the above comments, a promotion should never be thrust upon an individual. It should be offered. Some people do not want to be promoted, particularly if the promotion involves a step up to supervisory responsibilities.

When offering the promotion, we recommend that you be prepared to present the entire package, including salary, title, additional benefits, and a description of the new position. We are constantly amazed at how often just the opposite is done, and people are promoted to positions of increased responsibility without being told what the new compensation package consists of. No company would make an offer to an outsider without first providing the salary, title, benefits, and job description. Yet for promotions from within, this is frequently what happens. It's easy to understand why this is demotivating. It makes the individuals being promoted feel less valuable than new people coming into the organization.

CONCLUSIONS

Promotions are one of the key tools available to managers for motivating people, and motivating people is an important element of effective leadership. This chapter discussed two important aspects of a good promotion system—selecting those individuals qualified for promotion, and properly managing the promotion process. Establishing appropriate promotion selection criteria and assessing how candidates meet these requirements are key elements of an effective promotion selection process. Management of the promotion process also requires confidentiality, elimination of promotion inequities, proper presentation of the promotion, and maintenance of individual dignity.

Further Reading

Hallenberg, E. X., "Dual Advancement Ladder Provides Unique Recognition for the Scientist," *Research Management*, Vol. 13, No. 3, 1970.

Bowman, Garda W., "What Helps or Harms Promotability?" *Harvard Business Review*, January-February, 1964, No. 64102.

Francis, Philip H., *Principles of R&D Management*, American Management Associations, 1977.

Fader, Shirley Sloan, "Getting Promoted—Making Your Own Good Luck," *Careers*, McGraw-Hill, April 1987.

Koontz, Harold, and O'Donnell, Cyril, *Principles of Management*, McGraw-Hill Book Company, 1968.

Chapter 7
COUNSELLING

John Mahl was upset with Charlie Padosian. He had talked to Charlie several times about the low quality of his trip reports. As a district sales manager for an auto parts distributor, John relied heavily on the written reports his six sales people wrote concerning new sales prospects. Most of the six were on the road at any given time, so John needed the reports to determine where to focus his group's efforts, and to make recommendations to his boss about what parts, and how many, should be kept in stock. The latest report Charlie had written was typical, and reflected the problems John had observed in Charlie's other reports. It simply stated whom he had visited, without any conclusions or recommendations. John called Charlie into his office.

"Charlie, I thought we had an understanding about these trip reports," John said.

"Yes, we do," Charlie said. "I visited seventeen stores in the last two days. Fourteen are already buying from us, and the other three are new. Two of those three ordered about a thousand dollars worth of loose tools. The other fourteen placed their standard orders. Nothing new with those guys, more or less."

"That's good," John said. "I didn't realize you had hit so many stores, but we still need to talk about these trip reports."

"The tool orders were pretty good," Charlie said. "We haven't been moving too much of that stuff, but with the new tools we've been buying from Japan, the markup's pretty good. You know, a lot of people are doing their own auto work these days. It's a lot different than it was fifteen, even ten years ago."

"Do you think we could increase the tool volume to other stores in the district?" John asked.

"Maybe," Charlie answered. "Like I said, a lot more people. . . ."

Just then, one of the other salesmen stuck his head in the door. "Hey, Charlie, there's a call for you at my desk."

"Okay," Charlie said, getting up to leave. "We can talk about the tools a little more later on, John. Gotta go."

Charlie left and John stared at his desk. He wasn't sure what had transpired until he heard the two departing salesmen as they walked away.

"What did he want?" asked the one.

"Beats me," Charlie said. "Just wanted to talk about tool orders, I guess."

***

Providing feedback through counselling is one of the best ways to improve the performance of your subordinates, if the counselling is done in an effective manner. Many managers assume their subordinates know if they are performing up to par, but making such an assumption is often a mistake. Your subordinates won't know what you think of their performance unless you tell them.

Counselling is not easy, and most managers (including both experienced and inexperienced managers) don't do it very well. For example, have you ever counselled someone and felt you might not have gotten your point across (as obviously occurred in the example above)? Did the employee's subsequent behavior later confirm your suspicions? Have you, as a subordinate, ever left a meeting wondering if the boss was displeased with your performance because of some vague remarks he or she made?

The reasons for these uncertainties are simple. People generally hear what they want to hear, especially if what they don't want to hear is couched in vague language. So they miss the message. Unfortunately, it's easy to be vague when discussing poor performance. The result is poor communication and ineffective counselling.

A RECOMMENDED APPROACH TO COUNSELLING

As is the case for most management activities, counselling can be broken down into a series of decisions and actions:

- deciding if counselling is required;
- scheduling the counselling session;
- preparing for the counselling session;
- conducting the counselling session;
- assessing if the counselling was effective.

The flow chart shown here illustrates this process.

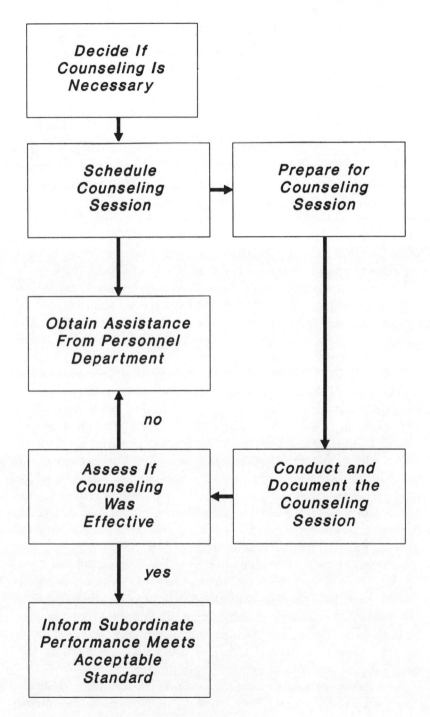

Figure 7–1. The counselling process.

DECIDING IF
COUNSELLING
IS REQUIRED

In order to decide if counselling is required, you must first apply a standard to the work being done. A standard is a set of established criteria that can be used in an objective and consistent manner to judge performance. It's important to recognize that you may not be the best person to establish the standard, even if you used to do the same job. After all, you didn't get to be a manager by being slow or doing average work. A far better standard by which to judge performance is to compare the performance to that of others doing similar work.

If you are not certain that the standard is well understood by your subordinates, give them the benefit of the doubt. Explain what you expect first, and then give your subordinates a chance to meet your expectations. Our experience indicates that substandard work is often the result of not knowing the standard.

Once you and your subordinates have a clear understanding of the standard, it will be easier to judge if it has been met. But how big must the gap be between performance and standard to justify counselling? This decision is subjective, and will depend a great deal on your management style and the type of work being performed.

Consider two examples to illustrate this point. Suppose one of your subordinates exceeds a budget by a small amount. If the overrun is not too significant, counselling would probably do more harm than good. In this case, neither the frequency nor the consequences of the overrun present a serious problem. However, if this problem occurred frequently, counselling may be required.

Suppose another subordinate performed well technically on a project, but finished the project several days late. In this case, missing the deadline may have serious implications, particularly if there is a financial penalty or customer dissatisfaction. The problem may be compounded if the delinquency was a surprise (perhaps you found out the day the work was due). If either of the above conditions is true, counselling is probably warranted.

To consider one more example, suppose the problem described above occurred because you assigned additional tasks to the subordinate without considering the impact. The subordinate should have notified you that a schedule slip would result, but based on our experience, subordinates are frequently reluctant to do so. In this case, you were at least partly the cause of the missed commitment, and the need for counselling becomes less certain.

The point is that you must consider the *consequences*, *causes*, and *frequency* of not meeting the standard to decide if counselling is required. If you counsel for every minor deficiency, your group will develop a serious morale problem. On the other hand, if you fail to provide counselling when it is needed, you may soon have a group of happy nonperformers. Sensitivity to these thresholds (that is, deciding when counselling is required) comes with experience. If your initial attempts to define the thresholds are based on the guidelines described above (i.e., if you consider the consequences, causes, and frequency of not meeting a standard), less time will be required to gain this experience.

SCHEDULING THE COUNSELLING SESSION

The next decision you have to make is whether counselling should be done immediately or scheduled for a later time. Immediate counselling is recommended for minor problems, but always make sure you take your subordinate aside and do it privately (we'll talk more about the importance of private counselling later).

Counselling for more serious or recurring problems should be scheduled for a later time. This delay will give both you and your subordinate time to prepare. Do not delay the counselling session too long, though. Lengthy delays tend to disassociate counselling from the performance you wanted to address. They also produce unnecessary anxiety.

If you choose to delay the counselling session, you need to inform your subordinate of your plans to provide counselling. Informing a subordinate of the planned counselling session will, in itself, be perceived as negative counselling. For this reason, you should tell the subordinate of the time, location, and subject privately. Avoid a manner or tone of voice that expresses dissatisfaction, and don't be pulled into conducting the counselling session itself at the time you inform your subordinate. If the subordinate tries to insist on discussing the issues immediately, simply say that you will be better prepared at the scheduled time.

PREPARING FOR THE COUNSELLING SESSION

Outline in writing the points you want to cover before the counselling session. Counselling sessions are usually emotional experiences, and in such an environment, it's easy to forget major issues. Notes help to prevent that.

Think about the location and seating arrangement. If your office doesn't have a door, find a room that does. Where you sit will also affect the message you want to transmit. Sitting on opposite sides of the desk is formal, and appropriate for serious issues. Sitting alongside the subordinate often lessens the emotional and confrontational aspects of the counselling session.

CONDUCTING THE COUNSELLING SESSION

Counselling is a difficult and delicate management task, but timing and preparation make the task easier. In conducting the session, the following guidelines will also help:

- Get to the point, and don't be abstract in your discussions. As mentioned earlier, most people hear what they want to hear. If you're not straightforward in your discussion of a performance deficiency, your subordinate will probably leave the counselling session without realizing a performance improvement is required.
- Always conduct the counselling session privately. Criticizing a subordinate in front of others is one of the worst things a manager can do. Public criticism is embarrassing and discouraging. It also obscures your message, and causes observers to lower their opinions of you. If you make it a habit to counsel privately, your subordinates will appreciate your sensitivity to their feelings, and accept you as a manager more quickly.
- Never display emotion. A display of emotion on your part will undermine your authority, obscure your message, and can lead to confrontations. Even if the subordinate becomes emotional or confrontational, stick to the issues in an objective manner.
- Allow the subordinate an opportunity to respond to your concerns. Ask for his or her opinions on the cause of the problem. You may discover legitimate obstacles preventing the subordinate from

meeting required standards. If this turns out to be the case, you will look much better if you are objective and not emotional.

• Develop a plan with your subordinate to correct deficiencies. If you allow your subordinate to take the major role in developing the plan, he or she will probably do a better job adhering to it. Make sure the plan has goals for improvement, with a deadline for achieving each goal.

• If possible, close the counselling session on a positive note. Find something good about the employee's performance, and finish the session by mentioning it.

After the counselling session, document the key points of your discussion. It's not necessary to give a copy of this record to your subordinate, but it's important that you keep it. You need a record to assure objectivity when evaluating subsequent performance. Documenting counselling is also important for legal reasons, should further action be necessary (such as reassignment or termination).

The approach outlined here elevates the counselling session from a mere scolding to a meaningful exchange of information designed to help correct performance deficiencies. The meeting focuses on bringing problems to light, developing a plan for corrective action, and giving the subordinate responsibility for improving performance. This last issue is critically important. The objectives of successful counselling are to reveal unsatisfactory performance, and to delegate responsibility for improvement.

ASSESSING COUNSELLING EFFECTIVENESS

Once the counselling session is over, you need to follow up by observing your subordinate's performance. Measure performance against the plan developed in the previous step, and let your subordinate know how he or she is doing. If the performance has improved, say so. If the problems persist, however, you will need to conduct additional counselling sessions and continue to document the results.

It's a good idea to involve someone from the personnel department for such additional sessions. If there is no meaningful performance improvement after several counselling sessions, reassignment or termination is probably necessary. The personnel department knows how to handle this without getting you or your company in trouble.

Further Reading

Hunsaker, Philip L., and Allesandra, Anthony J., *The Art of Managing People*, Prentice-Hall, Inc., 1980.

Steers, R. M., and Porter, L. W., "The Role of Task-Goal Attributes in Employee Performance," *Psychological Bulletin*, Vol. 81, 1974.

Lewis, Philip V., and Williams, John, *Readings in Organizational Communication*, Grid Publishing Company, 1980.

Blanchard, Kenneth, and Johnson, Spencer, *The One Minute Manager*, William Morrow and Company, Inc., 1982.

Chapter 8
APPRAISALS AND REVIEWS

The previous chapter discussed techniques for effective counselling. There the emphasis was on correcting performance deficiencies as they developed. Along with these "as-required" counselling sessions, there are two other important instruments a manager can use to provide valuable feedback to subordinates: performance appraisals and salary reviews.

Many companies, particularly smaller ones, don't use performance appraisals at all. Based on our observations, many of the companies that use performance appraisals administer them poorly. Our experience also shows that salary reviews are generally handled somewhat better than performance appraisals, but problems frequently develop in this area, too.

These deficiencies are unfortunate, because performance appraisals and salary reviews can be valuable tools. When administered fairly, they can do much to improve substandard performance and encourage superior performance.

An example of what can go wrong if performance appraisals and salary reviews are not properly administered may be found in the case of Jack B., a newly promoted supervisor. Shortly after being promoted to his supervisory position, Jack was directed by the boss to "get rid of the deadwood" in his section. Jack hadn't had time to really get to know the people in his new group, so he asked the group's former supervisors for their opinions. Jack also solicited the opinions of several other supervisors. These discussions consistently identified one individual (a man who had been with the company for more than twenty years) as a poor performer. Jack interviewed each of the people in his new group, and found they generally felt the same way. After he talked to the man in question, Jack formed the same opinion. The man had a cavalier attitude, admitted that he spent much of the day on the phone with his stockbroker, and clearly placed little emphasis on the requirements of his job.

Jack talked to his boss, and was directed to make the necessary arrangements to terminate the man. When Jack talked to the personnel supervisor, things fell apart. The man's records were examined, and the personnel supervisor told Jack "there's no way we can terminate him."

"I don't understand," Jack said. "Everyone I've talked with says this guy's a dud. What's the problem?"

"The problem," said the personnel supervisor, "is that this guy probably is an absolute zero, but you can't tell it from this." He pushed the man's personnel file to Jack. "Just look through it. He's got over twenty years' worth of performance appraisals in here. None of them say a single negative thing. Average to above average ratings. Average raises the whole time. If we terminated him, he'd be a fool not to sue us for wrongful discharge. His personnel file would be examined in court, and he'd walk out owning this place."

Jack explained the problem to his boss, and they called in the group's two former supervisors, one of whom had been promoted to a middle-management position. Without explaining the details, Jack's boss asked each for their opinions. They both said the man was a marginal performer. Jack's boss then asked why they had given him average performance reviews and raises. Neither of the former supervisors answered. Finally, the one who had been promoted (and was now at the same level as Jack's boss) responded. "You knew the guy was a dud as well as we did," he said, "and you signed those raises and reviews. . . ."

***

The point of this story is that performance appraisals and salary reviews are not to be taken lightly. Giving average raises and performance appraisals to poor performers is unfair to other people in the company. It's also unfair to the company itself, for the reasons shown above.

The above example focused on one of the negative aspects of poorly administering salary and performance reviews. When these reviews are properly performed, however, they offer many advantages.

PERFORMANCE APPRAISALS

Our experience leads us to believe that there are few management tasks more difficult than sitting down with another human being to discuss his or her strengths and weaknesses. For all of the reasons discussed in the chapter on counselling, the experience is a humbling one for both the manager and the subordinate. All of the techniques discussed in the previous chapter are applicable here. These include establishing the proper environment, seating arrangements, and privacy, among other things.

In the chapter on counselling, much of the emphasis was on correcting performance deficiencies. We recommended those sessions be done on an as-required basis, as it's not a good idea to wait until a scheduled formal performance review (which might be months away) to discuss any serious deficiencies. Performance appraisals are not only for documenting areas where improvement is required, however. The appraisal is also a powerful vehicle for reinforcing positive behavior. Our experience shows that documenting a subordinate's strengths is a positive motivator, and tends to fulfill one's need for self-actualization. According to Hitt, a management consultant and author, reinforcing positive performance characteristics can be a particularly powerful motivator when the individual's strengths are tied to organizational goals, as will be discussed below (Hitt, William D., "Management in Action," Battelle Press, 1985).

FORMAT

Performance appraisals are usually based on numerical rating schemes, qualitative assessments, or combinations of the two. We believe that numerical rating schemes are not very effective as evaluation tools, due primarily to the subjectivity of what purports to be an objective, quantitative rating method. Differences in job content and evaluators often make enormous differences in the way subordinates are evaluated.

We strongly encourage the use of goal-oriented performance appraisal systems. These systems have the manager and subordinate agree on objectives at the beginning of the appraisal period, and then evaluate progress towards meeting these objectives throughout the period. There are several advantages to this approach. By allowing the subordinate to participate in establishing objectives, it allows the subordinate to establish ownership in (and more enthusiastic acceptance of) organizational goals. Goal-oriented systems also encourage the subordinate to meet objectives, because he or she knows exactly what constitutes the basis for performance evaluation. This provides a sense of control over one's progress in the organization. Finally, even though this performance appraisal method is largely qualitative, it eliminates many of the subjectivity problems associated with quantitative, numerical rating schemes. The performance appraisal objectives are either met, or they are not.

FREQUENCY

Most business organizations conduct performance appraisals on a regularly scheduled annual basis. Limiting performance appraisals in this manner probably isn't a good idea. The military forces, for example, prepare performance appraisals annually, but they also review subordinate performance if the subordinate or supervisor is reassigned, or if the subordinate performs in a particularly exemplary, or particularly poor, manner. This approach inherently makes sense. Evaluations that recognize outstanding performance in a timely manner (instead of waiting until the end of the appraisal period) reinforce such behavior. Appraisals prepared when the subordinate or supervisor is reassigned eliminates the problem of evaluations prepared by managers who have little familiarity with the subordinate's work.

FAIRNESS

Fairness is key to the success of the performance appraisal, and above all else, performance appraisals must be fair. Perhaps more significantly, the subordinate being evaluated must perceive the appraisal to be fair. The appraisal may be accurate and fair, but if the subordinate does not recognize this, the appraisal will probably serve only to demotivate the individual. There are two dimensions to the fairness issue. The first is consistency, i.e., don't criticize a deficiency in one subordinate while accepting it in another. The second is allowing the subordinate an opportunity to correct a problem before documenting it (as was discussed in the chapter on counselling).

The appraisal will be fair (and will probably be perceived by the subordinate as fair) if you use examples to support your conclusions. These examples should be based on the subordinate's performance during the appraisal period. Examples help the manager determine what the performance appraisal should say. They also help the subordinate understand the basis for the appraisal. Examples serve one final purpose, and that's to make the performance appraisal defensible. Suppose you wrote a negative performance appraisal for a subordinate, with no examples to support your conclusions. If that subordinate goes to your boss or the personnel department to complain about an unfair review, what will you be able to offer as a defense for what you wrote?

SALARY REVIEWS

According to Kevin J. Murphy (an expert in the field of compensation), salary administration is an emotional issue. The reasons are obvious. A manager can send no stronger signal to the subordinate concerning his or her worth to the organization. There is no other action (short of termination) that has as direct an influence on the subordinate's standard of living. Although the evidence is not conclusive, many compensation experts (including Murphy) contend that there is a correlation between pay increases and performance, and between pay increases and value to the organization. For these reasons, it's even more important that the administration of pay increases be handled in a fair and proper manner.

One might expect this to be more of a problem in small companies, where pay increases are largely left to the discretion of the owner or manager, but big companies have their problems, too. For example, secretarial pay increases in many large companies are based on a six-month review cycle, with the extremes of the increase based on a very narrow spread (i.e., the range from the minimum to the maximum raise). Fifty to seventy dollars per month is common, with a marginal secretary receiving a fifty dollar raise, an exceptional secretary receiving a seventy dollar raise, and an average secretary receiving a sixty dollar raise. The problem is that an extra ten dollars per month provides very little additional incentive.

Much the same holds true for professional salary increases, although managers generally have a little more freedom to recognize differences between subordinates. Larger organizations usually distribute a merit pool each year. Some compensation experts argue that the term "merit" is incorrect, and that such raises are actually cost-of-living adjustments. We tend to agree, but our experience shows this to be the case only when salary administration is poorly handled. The problem we've seen is that the annual pool is frequently tied to the general inflation level, and most managers tend to give raises that are very close to the pool percentage. If the pool were 6 percent (as is typical these days), a strong contributor might get a 7 percent increase, while a marginal performer might get 5 percent. The problem becomes the same as that described for secretaries. Many people won't go the extra mile for an extra 1 percent increase.

The remainder of this chapter will discuss methods for identifying those who deserve above average, average, and below average increases, and how to get the most mileage from these increases. It's important to recognize that in order for the increase to have meaning, the manager has to be willing to differentiate among subordinate levels of performance, and financially recognize these differences in a significant manner. If this is not done, you might as well give everyone the same raise. We knew a supervisor who did just that for several years, with predictable results. The better performers left the group, its performance deteriorated, and, ultimately, the manager was reassigned to a non-managerial position.

DETERMINING SALARY INCREASES

There are basically three methods to determine salary increases. These include the use of totem ranking schemes, consideration of demonstrated performance, and comparison to industry standards.

Totem ranking schemes determine each employee's raise based on the manager's perception of the employee's value to the organization, and the employee's current salary. The system requires listing each employee in the order of their perceived value to the group in a vertical fashion (hence the "totem" description), and then plotting their current salaries along a horizontal axis. An example of this is shown in Figure 8–1. Ideally, the line formed by connecting the employees' salaries should extend upwards and to the right, with no serious discontinuities. Where such breaks occur, the merit budget should be allocated to correct the discontinuity (or at least move towards correcting the discontinuity, if the discontinuity is too large to correct in one year). This can be seen in the case of Wil Martin, who is ranked second in the group. Martin's salary is lower than those ranked third and fourth, so the allocation of increases should move to correct this inequity.

A second method of allocating merit increases is to base each individual's raise on their demonstrated performance during the appraisal period. The concept works better when the merit allocation is supported by a goal-oriented performance appraisal system, as described earlier in this chapter. There are a couple of problems with this system, though. One is that it depends on the appropriateness of the goals established in the performance appraisal. If the goals are trivial, then the employee might expect a maximum salary increase for meeting a set of meaningless objectives. Another problem is that this approach fails to take the relative value of each employee into account (as does the totem ranking scheme).

The third method for determining salary increases is to evaluate how well the people in your group are being paid compared to others in the

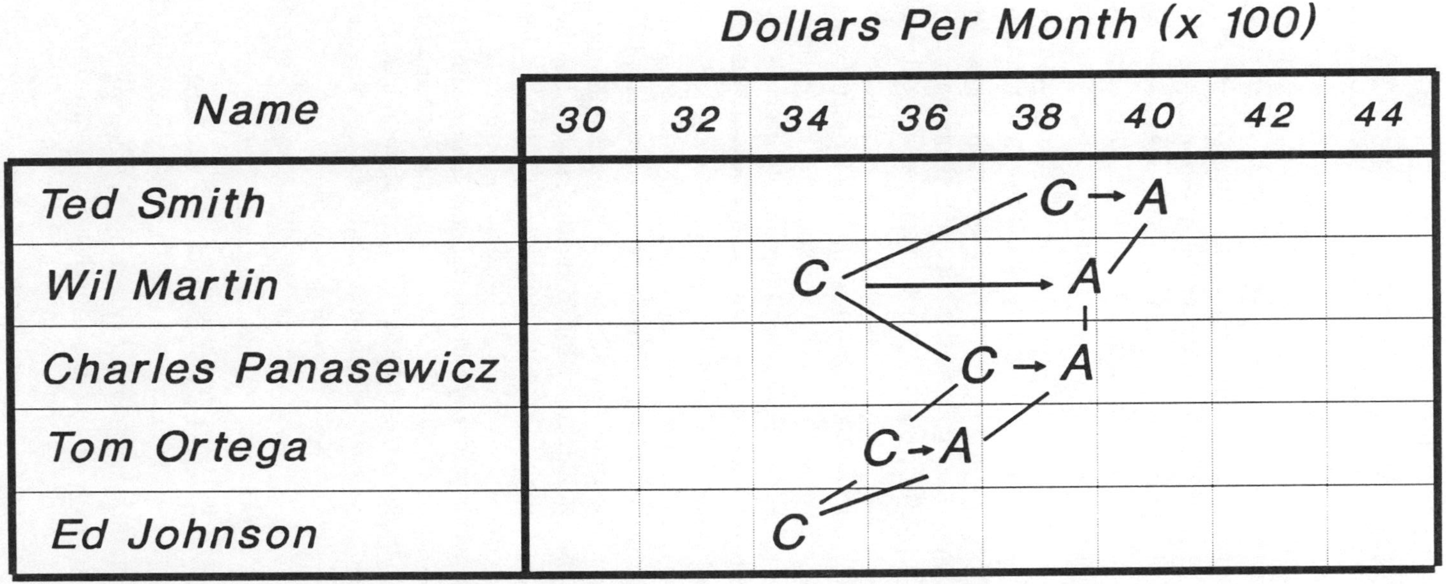

Dollars Per Month (x 100)

Name	30	32	34	36	38	40	42	44
Ted Smith					C→A			
Wil Martin			C		A			
Charles Panasewicz				C→A				
Tom Ortega				C→A				
Ed Johnson			C					

Figure 8–1. An example of a totem scheme for determining salary increases. The group members are ranked (from top to bottom) in order of their relative value to the organization. Current salaries are represented by a "C" and the amount after the increase is represented by an "A." The idea is that a line formed by connecting the salaries should extend upwards and to the right, with no serious discontinuities. Where discontinuities occur, as is the case for Wil Martin, the increase should be large enough to reflect his value to the organization. Due to his relative value, Martin receives the largest raise. In this merit budget allocation, Johnson receives no increase, consistent with his low ranking.

industry. The idea is that if people are paid less than those doing similar work for other companies, the merit pool should be adjusted to achieve equity. Larger companies usually have personnel departments that can perform this evaluation. Managers in smaller companies may have to rely on other sources of information. Your counterparts at other companies are often a good source. When asked what they pay their employees, other managers are frequently (and, at least to us, surprisingly) willing to divulge this information. Your subordinates are another good source of information. Subordinates are often aware of what competitors are paying, and if your people leave the organization to work for higher salaries, an adjustment is required.

We believe the best approach is to incorporate all three methods described above when allocating salary increases. The totem ranking scheme gives a good overview of relative value to the organization, but it would be unfair to give a large increase to someone high on the totem simply because of value (if the person had not met his or her goals for the year, for example, they probably do not deserve a large increase). Industry standards must also be taken into account. If a large increase keeps a person below what could be earned working for a competitor, adjustments are required. For these reasons, blending all three assessment methods often provides a more equitable merit increase allocation, and recognizes the larger needs of the organization.

Presenting the raise to the subordinate should be done with as much care as counselling or administering a performance appraisal. The presentation should be scheduled in advance, and performed privately. You should allow enough time to explain the reasons for the amount to the subordinate (here's where examples will help), and for the subordinate to ask questions. We've both seen and experienced instances in which a supervisor simply handed the raise to the subordinate, with no explanation as to the amount. This is a poor approach, as it tells the subordinate that the manager cares very little about recognizing superior performance. It's far better to treat the salary increase with the significance it deserves.

CONCLUSIONS

Performance appraisals and salary increases are probably the two most important motivators available to a manager. Both are frequently emotionally charged issues, both for the manager and the subordinate. When used properly, both are important instruments to recognize and document above- and below-average performance. For these reasons, it's important that performance appraisals and salary increases be handled in a professional, equitable, and defensible manner.

Further Reading

Hitt, William D., *Management in Action*, Battelle Press, 1985.

Murphy, Kevin J., "Top Executives Are Worth Every Nickel They Get," *Harvard Business Review*, March-April 1986.

Beer, Michael; Spector, Bert; Lawrence, Paul; Mills, D. Quinn; and Walton, Richard E., *Human Resource Management: A General Manager's Perspective*, The Free Press, 1985.

The Standard Manual for Supervisors, National Foreman's Institute, 1982.

Lawrence, Paul R., and Lorsch, Jay W., *Organization and Environment*, Richard D. Irwin, Inc., 1969.

Chapter 9

TERMINATIONS

Ed Ashbough felt uneasy about the upcoming meeting. He had counseled Dolores Haney repeatedly during the last several weeks concerning her attitude towards the customers. Ed worked for a large supermarket chain. He was the assistant manager at one of the stores, and in fact, was the man in charge during the evening hours. Dolores worked at one of the check-out booths.

The problem started about two months ago, when one of the customers complained to Ed about Dolores' rude manner at the cash register. Dolores worked at the express check-out, where the customers were supposed to have no more than ten items. The initial complaint had been that Dolores made a biting comment to a woman with a full shopping cart. When Ed had talked with Dolores, she claimed that she had told the woman only shoppers with ten items or less were supposed to use the express line. Dolores denied that she had been rude.

About two weeks later, another customer saw Ed to complain about Dolores. Dolores again admitted she had pointed out the criteria for the express line. She also denied again that she had been rude. Dolores blamed the incident on the shopper. Ed explained to Dolores that she "had to be careful," and suggested that if she experienced another shopper in the express line with more than ten items, she should ignore it and allow the customer through. Dolores promised that she would.

About three evenings later, Ed happened to be near the express line and noticed a man in line with a full grocery cart. When the man got to Dolores, she said "I see you never learned to read."

Ed was astounded. He quietly stepped behind the register, finished the sale, and assigned another clerk. He motioned for Dolores to follow him to the office.

"I can't believe what I just heard," Ed said to Dolores. "How could you be so stupid? Didn't you understand the warnings I gave you before?"

Dolores started to answer, but Ed cut her off. "I really don't have time to listen to this," he said. "You're through. Gather your things, and get out. We'll mail you your last paycheck."

Dolores stared at the ground without saying anything for several seconds. She looked as if she might start to cry. Finally, she said "You can't treat me like this. I didn't know I was doing anything wrong, and if you fire me, I'll sue you and the company."

"Well, it's a free country, Dolores," Ed shot back. "You can do whatever you want."

When Ed came in the next day, he explained what had happened to his boss, the store manager, who sat and listened with a somber expression. Ed thought his boss was upset about Dolores being so rude to the customers.

"I didn't realize any of this was going on," the store manager said. "You didn't tell me anything, and I didn't see anything written down. Did you document your first two discussions with her?"

"No," Ed said. "I made it very clear, though, that . . ."

The store manager cut him off. "Did you discuss this with the employment people at corporate?"

"No," Ed said. He began to fidget, realizing that the store manager was upset all right, but not with Dolores.

"Did she say anything about the termination?" the store manager asked.

Ed recalled Dolores' remarks, and began to feel really uncomfortable. "Well, she said something about a lawsuit . . ." he mumbled.

The store manager picked up the phone and punched in a number. After a pause, he began speaking with someone on the other end, and Ed quickly realized it was the corporation's vice president of industrial relations. He looked at Ed and simply said, "You can go now."

As a manager, it's almost a certainty that sooner or later you will have to terminate someone. We've done it, and without question, administering a termination is the most distasteful managerial task one can experience. In today's legal environment, it's also one of the riskiest actions you or your company can take, particularly if proper termination procedures are not followed. In the example above, Ed probably had what appeared to be good grounds for terminating Dolores, but he did everything wrong. If Dolores followed through on her threat to pursue legal action, she would almost certainly win a wrongful discharge lawsuit. And according to an employment manager at a large manufacturing company, the average settlement for such lawsuits is $250,000.

THE TERMINATION DECISION

Perhaps the first question to consider is: When should someone be terminated? There are three answers. The first concerns the situation in which the job disappears, either through lack of business or reorganization. The second situation occurs when an individual commits an offense serious enough to warrant termination on the first offense. Although the criteria for this type of termination varies somewhat from company to company, typical offenses that might warrant termination on the first offense include theft, sexual harassment, physical assault, or serious safety violations.

The third situation, which is probably the most difficult when attempting to reach a termination decision, is the case in which an employee performs in a substandard manner and is unwilling or unable to improve. Although the techniques to be described for termination interviews in this chapter are applicable to all three types of terminations, most of the discussion here will be about arriving at a decision and administering a termination when faced with substandard performance.

Suppose you are faced with an employee who performs his or her job in a substandard manner. What should you do to correct the situation? Should you simply fire the offender? Should you discuss the areas of substandard performance verbally, and then, if no improvement results, terminate the offender? Should written notification be given first?

Our experience indicates that the best way to begin is to first discuss the issue with your boss. Whenever you counsel someone about substandard performance, there's a good chance the person will go over your head to see your boss, particularly if you are a new or young manager. If nothing else, it's a good idea to keep the boss informed so that he or she won't be surprised by such visits.

In order to protect both yourself and your company from litigation, and to be fair to the employee, you should objectively list the areas of substandard performance. Preferably, you should do this before you meet with the employee. The key here is objectivity. If your criticism is vague or otherwise nonspecific, you need to either better define your concerns, or else forget about counselling the employee (Chapter 7 discusses counselling techniques in detail).

Once you have objectively identified objective performance deficiencies, you should meet with the employee. Opinions vary on whether to document the results of an initial counselling session. Our experience indicates that the first counselling session should probably be verbal. If you document deficiencies everytime you meet with a subordinate to discuss performance improvements, your people will soon grow to fear and dislike you. If performance doesn't improve after the first verbal counselling session, however, documentation is probably required, and should be administered in accordance with the guidance of Chapter 7. If your company has a personnel department, we strongly recommend including them at this point. Personnel specialists are knowledgeable in the details and legalities of documenting performance deficiencies. These deficiencies should be presented to the employee, along with a list of actions required to demonstrate performance improvement, and the dates by which these actions should be accomplished. Usually, thirty to ninety days are allowed.

As discussed in Chapter 7, the next step is to follow up on the employee's performance, and assess progress against correcting the documented deficiencies. Our experience has been that in about half the cases, the employee's performance improves sufficiently and no further action is required. The other half of the time, though, little or no improvement is shown. When this is the case, a decision about termination should be jointly arrived at by you, your boss, and the personnel department. In no case should you proceed with a termination without the approval of your boss and the employment people.

PREPARATION

Five preparatory actions are required prior to the termination interview. The manager needs to gather all of the documentation that lead to the termination decision, such as performance appraisals, corrective action plans, or other evidence of performance counselling. Gathering the documentation helps the company to defend itself against potential wrongful discharge lawsuits. This first step also leads into the second step, which is to clearly define the reasons for the termination. We suggest putting the reasons on paper, and using these notes during the termination interview.

The third step and fourth steps are to be thoroughly familiar with the company's termination policies and procedures, and to include the personnel department and your boss in the decision process (as discussed earlier). When proceeding with or contemplating a termination, don't do anything on your own. The consequences of a mistake can be severe.

The final preparatory step is to define the severance package. Very few companies simply fire people, and then leave them to fend for themselves. We've observed that most organizations provide considerable termination benefits to ease the terminated individual's financial burden and anxieties. These benefits may include such things as outplacement assistance, use of the clerical staff for assistance in resume

preparation and reproduction, use of an office, psychological coun-
seling, and continuation of health insurance and salary for specified
periods of time. You should work with your management and the
personnel department to determine what this package will consist of
prior to the termination interview.

THE TERMINATION INTERVIEW

Once a coordinated decision has been made to proceed with a termination and the necessary preparatory steps have been taken, one needs to
prepare for the termination interview. The best place to start is by
reviewing the four goals of a termination interview. These goals are:

- to present the termination decision to the individual being
  terminated
- to maintain the individual's self-esteem
- to allay the individual's anxiety about the future
- to meet the legal requirements associated with the termination
  process.

Each of these are explained in further detail below.

Helping the individual to maintain self-esteem is particularly important. Under any circumstances, a termination is a crushing experience.
The individual will be faced with immediate concerns about his or her
financial security. Most people will react to the termination as an acute
rejection. All of the psychological implications of personal rejection can
emerge. It's important for the manager to recognize that nothing is
gained by exacerbating the situation with condemnations of the individual's competency or behavior, even if the termination resulted from
such deficiencies. You certainly need to explain the reasons for the
termination, but to do so in an angry-parent-to-wayward-child manner
does not serve the best interests of the individual, the company, or you.
At this point, you are presenting information, not scolding the individual being terminated. There are good reasons for taking this approach.

The interview should be conducted privately. Many companies prefer to do this at the end of the day, so that most of the other employees
will have gone home and the individual being terminated will be spared
any embarrassment. Some companies prefer to administer terminations over the lunch hour for the same reason. Some companies won't
do termination interviews on a Friday, because they feel it would ruin
the individual's weekend. Others prefer a Friday, with the feeling that
the individual will have time to overcome the initial shock, and can

begin an active job search the following Monday. Once again, we recommend talking to your boss and the personnel department to determine the best approach.

The actual interview should be conducted with professionalism and dignity. Use an office with a door, ask the individual to sit down, and clearly state that you have made a decision to effect a termination. Before proceeding, allow a few seconds of silence for the message to sink in, and then proceed with an explanation of how the decision was reached. We recommend that this not be done in an accusatory or condemnatory manner. It's best to talk about performance deficiencies or behavioral problems as detached things instead of attributing them to the individual being terminated. For example, instead of saying "your chronic lateness leaves me no choice but to terminate you," you should say something like "chronic lateness is a problem the company cannot condone."

Reactions to terminations vary widely, and are frequently unpredictable. Mild-mannered people may become confrontational, or perhaps even violent. Arrogant or tough people may withdraw, or even cry. If violence is suspected, solicit assistance from the personnel department. They may administer the termination, or have a security guard present. When faced with unpredictable reactions, we've found that the manager's best reaction is no reaction at all. Don't allow yourself to be pulled into a debate. If an individual begins to cry, wait for them to stop. Your responsibility is to communicate an irreversible decision to terminate the individual in a professional manner that maintains the individual's self-esteem.

Once this message has been communicated, you should present the severance package. Explain the package in as much detail as is necessary, but don't negotiate. If the individual wants his or her salary to be continued for a longer period, explain that the company has carefully assembled the termination package and no further benefits are available. Be polite, but firm.

Finish the interview with a few closing remarks. Either you or someone from the personnel or security department should stay with the individual while they clear out their work area, and then escort them to the door.

CONCLUSIONS

Terminations are not pleasant experiences. It's one of the toughest things a manager will ever have to do. If handled in a professional manner, though, the unpleasantness can be minimized.

It's important to recognize that due to today's legal environment, terminations can also present enormous financial risks to your company. If a termination decision is not fair, or if the termination interview is poorly handled, it's quite likely your company, and perhaps even you personally, will be sued.

These factors need to be kept in mind and should be used to help guide the termination process, but they should not be used as an excuse to delay or avoid necessary terminations. According to the personnel department manager in a large manufacturing company, many managers wait too long to terminate. The result is a loss of productivity, and a perception in others that management is willing to tolerate substandard performance or aberrant behavior. Either situation is bad.

Although unpleasant, terminations are sometimes necessary. As a responsible manager, you cannot turn away from such a need. Handling terminations in the manner described in this chapter will maximize the benefit to the organization, while simultaneously minimizing exposure to lawsuits and the emotional shock of those who are terminated.

Further Reading

Whitefield, Debra, "Counselors Can Help Ease the Trauma of Losing Job," *The Los Angeles Times*, September 20, 1987.

Beer, Michael; Spector, Bert; Lawrence, Paul R.; Mills, D. Quinn; and Walton, Richard E., *Human Resources Management*, The Free Press, 1985.

Hampton, David R.; Summer, Charles E.; and Webber, Ross A, *Organizational Behavior and the Practice of Management*, Scott, Foresman and Company, 1978.

Posner, Mitchell J., *Executive Essentials*, Avon Books, 1982.

Part III
CAREER BUILDING

Chapter 10
NETWORKING

Networks are groups of personal contacts one can use to help achieve career and business objectives. There are many kinds of networks. Some are internal to the organization, such as peers with whom one might discuss the corporate culture, acquaintances to whom one might turn in order to meet a specific business objective, or a senior manager from whom one might seek career guidance.

Other networks exist outside the company. Examples include people who have left the company, who oftentimes can help secure new business or provide information about career opportunities in other companies. Professional societies also form important networks, from which one can learn the latest technologies or other skills peculiar to a profession.

This chapter explores the concept of networking, and how it can be used to advantage. Our experience has been that belonging to a variety of networks, both inside and outside the company, can provide many advantages and greatly enhance one's success as a manager.

INTERNAL NETWORKS

Although many people may not recognize it, anyone who works in an organization belongs to a network. That's because organizations really have two structures—the formal organization depicted on the organization chart and informal organizations. The formal organization chart shows reporting relationships, departmental boundaries, and who the managers are. But in reality, the formal organization exists only on paper.

The real organization is informal. It is not shown on any organization chart. Informal organizations, however, are the ones by which companies operate. The reporting relationships are often quite different than those shown on formal organization charts. Nonetheless, everyone knows where he or she fits in the informal organization (including such things as who the other group members are, and who the boss really is). Membership in informal organizations is generally voluntary, and for this reason, members of informal organizations usually work well together.

Understanding the concept of the informal organization is important because it helps to clarify the concept of a network. The informal organization is, after all, a network used to facilitate getting the job done. People belong to informal organizations (within the context of the company's formal organizations) because they feel comfortable with the other members, and they know how to use the informal organization in order to accomplish objectives. That's what networks are all about.

More efficient communication is one of the biggest advantages the informal organization has over the formal organization. There are several reasons for this, but the predominant reason is perhaps best explained by M. J. Jackson, a management researcher and author. Jackson maintains that communications flow more easily in informal organizations because the members feel more comfortable with and are more accessible to each other.

The informal organization allows more direct communications for another reason, and that's because it circumvents cumbersome chains of command. For example, if one needs to communicate with someone outside the formal group, it's much easier to establish a direct communications link with that person, as opposed to working up and down through two formal chains of command. This difference in communication flows is shown in Figure 10–1.

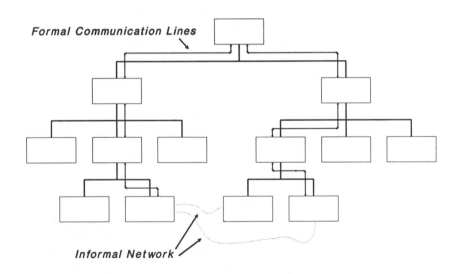

Figure 10–1. Flow of communications through the formal organization (solid line) versus flow of communications through an informal network (dashed line).

MENTORING

The internal networks discussed above are used to help one meet specific business objectives, such as finishing a proposal, coordinating a contract, or some other internal objective. There's another special kind of internal network. This network involves the concept of mentoring. A mentor is a senior manager who provides career and business guidance, usually to a more junior person. Mentor networks consist of only two people—the mentor and the person being offered the services of the mentor.

A mentor is essentially a business coach. Mentors can also be described as career consultants, with special insights due to position and familiarity with the organization. The mentor provides guidance to promising managers on how to best achieve business and career objectives.

We've observed that the best mentors are those who are not in the chain of command of those whom they are mentoring. In other words, if one were a manager in the accounting department, a mentor from the sales department is preferable to having the chief financial officer as a mentor. This practice is desirable for two reasons. It provides the younger manager advice from a broader perspective (i.e., outside the confines of one's own department). It also eliminates the inherent unfairness of an executive providing preferential subordinate guidance (i.e., helping the career of one subordinate, instead of all subordinates).

Initiating a mentor relationship calls for delicacy and diplomacy. One cannot approach a senior executive and simply ask for help in getting ahead. We recommend selecting someone outside one's chain of command, and with whom a degree of familiarity has been established (someone, perhaps, for whom you've worked in the past, or to whom you've had some other exposure). We have found that the best way to initiate a conversation that, hopefully, will lead to the development of a mentor is to approach the issue from the perspective of the mentor's success. Ask the prospective mentor how he or she advanced in the company. If approached with diplomacy in a relaxed, private setting, most executives are surprisingly willing to talk about themselves. Once the conversation is underway, the prospective mentor will probably begin to ask questions about your career aspirations. At the conclusion of the conversation, ask if you can return occasionally for additional guidance.

Mentoring is a complex subject. There are advantages and disadvantages to the practice. Obviously, those in the organization who don't have mentors may resent those who do. Mentoring raises serious questions about fairness and equal opportunity. We've never seen an organization with a formalized (or publicized) mentor program, but our experience indicates that these relationships exist in any large company. Franklin Lunding (former chief executive officer at Jewel Companies, an organization known for its young management) spoke very candidly about the practice. Lunding believes that anyone who breaks into the senior management ranks has had one or more mentors. Whether one agrees with the concept of mentoring or not, our experience supports Lunding's contention. We agree that if one wishes to continue to advance, developing a network that includes a mentor greatly enhances the probability of success.

EXTERNAL NETWORKS

Thus far, all of the networks discussed in this chapter have been internal (i.e., within the same business organization). External networks, or those that include contacts outside one's own company, can also provide powerful advantages.

Consider the example of Barney, a young engineer who worked for a company that designed and built computers for the Navy. Barney had been with the company as an engineer for about five years, and he wanted to become a manager. Barney talked to his boss, who told him that he was well-qualified for promotion to a management spot, but that no management positions were currently open. Barney's boss explained that the company had enough work to keep it going, but little new business was coming in, and none of the other managers were near retirement. There simply were no positions available.

Barney's company frequently retained an engineering consultant, however, to analyze electrical hazards on a new computer system. Barney's assignments required him to work with the consultant, and the two became good friends. Barney explained his desire to move into management. The consultant's advice to Barney was simple.

"Look, Barney," he said, "you're good at what you do, and you've got the right stuff to be a manager. But it won't happen here. Unless these guys get some new business soon, you and a lot of other people may not even have a job, let alone a manager's job. The only way you'll get into management here is if someone quits, gets fired, or dies, or if the company gets a major new contract. The marketing guys haven't done anything dramatic in the last three or four years, so you can forget about new business. And when's the last time anybody quit or got fired? I've been consulting here, off and on, for over five years, and I've never seen it happen. You've either got to accept a waiting period that may take years or find another company that needs your skills. It's that simple."

Barney thought about what the consultant said. "I've been thinking the same thing," Barney said, "but I haven't seen any ads for managers with my skills."

"You usually won't," the consultant said. "Those positions aren't usually advertised."

"So what do you do?" Barney asked.

"Well, there are a lot of things you can do," the consultant continued, "and one of them is to develop a network of contacts who know about these kinds of openings. Now, you know that as a consultant, I work for six or seven different companies. If I recruited people away from them, I'd have a hard time getting any future work. On the other hand, some of these outfits need people from time to time, and they ask me for recommendations. I'll keep you in mind."

Within a few weeks, the consultant learned of a management position (in Barney's area of expertise) opening up at another company. As the consultant had mentioned, the company did not intend to advertise the position. The consultant asked Barney to send a résumé to the hiring manager. The consultant also told the hiring manager about Barney, provided a good reference, and told the manager to expect the résumé. Within days, two interviews took place, and an offer was negotiated. Not long afterward, Barney had a new job as an engineering manager.

That wasn't the end of the association, though. Barney had more work than people, and he needed help. He contracted with the same consultant for a significant number of assignments. The consultant also helped Barney locate and hire the engineers he needed. The association between Barney and the consultant has continued for years, providing benefits to both men.

DEVELOPING NETWORKS

There are many kinds of internal and external networks, and belonging to networks provides a competitive advantage. But how does one develop a network?

One way to rapidly get tuned into a network is to join a professional association. The networks you can tie into in professional associations are good sources of information on which companies are hiring, which ones are laying off, which are the best-paying, and what the latest technological, managerial, or sales developments are. Professional associations allow people working in the same field to develop contacts with their counterparts in other companies. Professional societies generally have regular meetings, and many have annual symposiums. These meetings offer excellent opportunities to develop and maintain professional contacts. Professional associations also offer other advantages, such as exposure to the latest technologies, camaraderie, and opportunities for professional development.

There are several ways to learn about professional societies. Other people in your company will probably know about them. You can also identify professional associations by examining periodicals in your field of interest. The library is a good place to start.

In addition to joining professional associations, there are many other ways to develop contacts. You can develop a network simply by getting to know your counterparts in other companies. Trade shows also offer opportunities to expand your circle of contacts, as do classes and seminars. Professional recruiters can also be valuable contacts. Interviews are another good way to expand one's circle of contacts. These contacts can include people who interview you, and people you interview, even if an offer isn't extended or accepted. It's not at all uncommon to be turned down for one job, for example, and subsequently be invited back to interview for another. It's also quite common to use the contacts made during an interview for other business purposes.

The key idea in developing networks is to increase the number of people one knows. A very successful manager (who later became a company president) put this into perspective when he explained:

> "When I first worked in marketing, I used to hate all of the travelling my job required. One day I made a decision to use each trip as an opportunity to meet at least one new person, to remember who that person was, and to maintain contact (even if only on an infrequent basis) with that person. That was one of the smartest things I ever did. I started to enjoy the trips more, and now I have thousands of contacts—potential customers, people who can put me in contact with potential customers, potential employers, potential employment candidates, and so on. . . ."

The importance of meeting and cultivating contacts cannot be over-emphasized. Companies don't usually advertise management positions, or critical material needs, or other special requirements. With greater numbers of contacts, though, the probability of learning about these opportunities ahead of the competition rises dramatically.

THE ETHICS OF NETWORKING

From some perspectives, networks have a bad reputation. Our experience shows that many younger employees, and some newer managers, dismiss networks as political contrivances. Before using the stigma of "politics" to legitimize any negative feelings about networks, however, one must examine his or her definition of politics. If one defines politics as knowing and being able to influence the right people in order to achieve objectives, then (at least in our opinion) networks are a positive thing.

Consider, for example, the phenomenon of so-called "old boy" networks. Old boy networks are generally perceived to be a collection of male cronies, presumably at least middle-aged, who hold the real decision-making power in the organization. The perception further holds that this power is generally used (at least partially) to promote negative objectives.

An old boy network might not be such a bad thing, however. The old boys who belong to it, for example, probably feel their association is a very good thing, both for themselves and for the company. If the old boys support each other to develop new sales, recruit new talent for the organization, or to generally help the company run smoothly and profitably, then the old boy network is a good thing (at least for the old boys, and probably for the company as well). It's all a question of perspective, and what the network can do for its members.

CONCLUSIONS

Networks provide many advantages for their members, but without question, the most important advantage is access to information. R. Michels (a management researcher who did his work in the early part of this century) was one of the first modern students of management to assert that information is power. With the latest and most accurate information, a manager has the ability to influence his or her surroundings. This gives one decided advantages in being prepared to seize opportunities, avoid pitfalls, and attain greater success. Networks facilitate the process by providing access to information. The best way to develop networks is to meet people, and then to maintain these contacts. Networking can provide all of the advantages described in this chapter, along with the satisfaction of increasing your circle of friends.

Further Reading

Jackson, M. J., "The Organization and Its Communication Problem," *Communications for Management*, Scott, Foresman, 1969.

Michels, R., *Political Parties*, Dover Publications, 1959 (originally published in 1915).

"Everyone Who Makes It Has A Mentor," *Harvard Business Review*, July–August 1978, No. 78403.

Lunding, Franklin J., *Sharing a Business*, Updegraff Press, Ltd., 1954.

Connor, Robert J., "The Killer Instinct," *Careers*, McGraw-Hill, 1987.

Chapter 11
WRITING

Writing is one of the key means by which managers communicate in the business world (the other is speaking, which will be covered in Chapter 12). Because of the relative permanence of a business document, writing is an almost irrevocable competence indicator. When reading a well-written piece of business correspondence or documentation, our experience is that one forms an immediate favorable impression of the writer.

On the other hand, have you ever read a poorly written document and not formed a negative opinion of the writer? There's a message here, and it's that writing is one of the key discriminators by which you'll be judged. For that reason (as well as others to be discussed later), success as a manager is strongly linked to one's ability to write effectively. Effective writing must be clear, concise, free of grammatical and spelling errors, and accurate.

The requirement for clarity and conciseness becomes even more important when the schedules of key decision-makers are considered. Early in our careers, we've felt the urge to write lengthy reports and voluminous documents, probably as much to impress ourselves as our readers. For a very simple reason, however, this approach doesn't work in the business world. If your message isn't succinctly stated in the first few sentences, your writing will most likely end up in the wastebasket. Senior managers, in particular, have vast responsibilities and little time. When preparing business correspondence, remember that you are not writing a mystery novel. You can't take the reader on an interesting (at least to you) journey through a long-winded discourse, and then (maybe) reveal the main points in the last paragraph. Yet, we've found that much of the business correspondence and documentation we read suffers from exactly this problem. If the message isn't immediately apparent, our experience indicates it will not be communicated.

To put the importance of effective writing in perspective, consider the fields of engineering and science. This area is quantitative, highly technical, and often hardware-oriented. One might assume the need for effective writing skills is not as great as it might be in, say, marketing, advertising, strategic planning, or some other less-technical area. Yet, according to John Brogan, a management consultant specializing in technical writing, engineers and scientists spend more than half their time writing. Their managers spend even more time writing. If this is the case in an area where much of the work is quantitative (and often hands-on), the percentage of time spent writing by professionals in other areas must be even higher. The need for effective writing is obvious.

THE PROCESS OF BUSINESS WRITING

As is true for management activities, writing is a process, and as such it can be described in a flow chart. Figure 11–1 shows four steps: identifying the message, getting the key ideas down on paper, developing an outline, and writing the document. This sounds simple, yet our experience shows that it is often not followed, and more often than not, writing that is extremely difficult or impossible to understand is the result. Sometimes the outcome is almost comical. We've experienced instances in which the authors of business documents, when reading them at a later date, could not tell us what the documents meant. Suppose such a document went to a customer as a business proposal. Would it inspire confidence, or induce a potential customer to do business with you?

IDENTIFYING THE MESSAGE

Perhaps the most important step in effective business writing is identifying the message to be communicated. Our feeling is that if you can't state the message in a single sentence, you probably haven't spent enough time attempting to understand what you want to communicate. And if you don't understand the message, it's almost a certainty that your readers will be confused. To define the message, we recommend asking two questions:

What message do you want to communicate?
What do you hope to accomplish by communicating this message?

Although these questions may seem trivial, they are not. Think about the number of times you've read business correspondence and wondered what the writing was trying to say, and why.

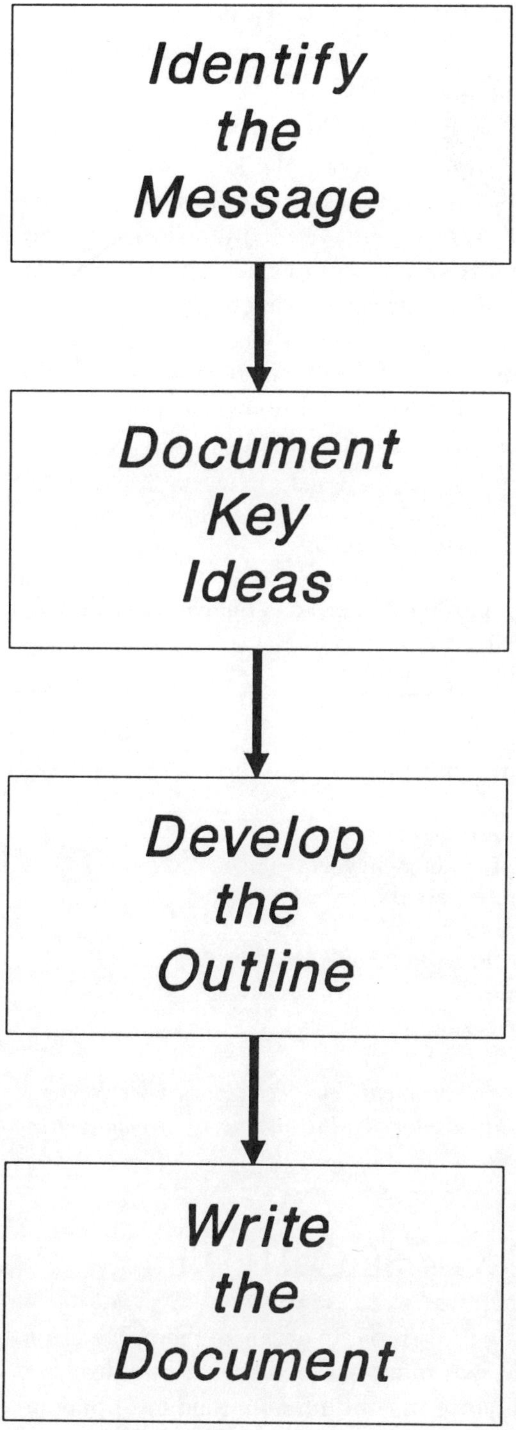

Identify
the
Message

Document
Key
Ideas

Develop
the
Outline

Write
the
Document

Figure 11–1. The process of
producing an effective written
document.

DOCUMENTING KEY IDEAS

During the process of developing the key message, we recommend listing all related thoughts. We've found that the key message will emerge during this process. After identifying the key thoughts, note any sub-points and supporting information. Putting these in the right order isn't important just yet. At this point, you're brainstorming, and you want to capture all thoughts on paper. In fact, it's important that you not take time to organize these ideas yet. That might interrupt or distract the brainstorming process, which should be focused on identifying points necessary to support the major thrust of your writing. To better illustrate this process, a list of ideas is shown in Figure 11–2 (these were the ones developed to write this chapter).

—**Bubble chart outline**
—**Get major message across in first few words**
   (executive summary)
—**Get rough ideas down on paper first—then go to bubble chart outline**
—**Include flow chart in narrative**
—**Be conversational (not stilted)—be natural**
—**key things/phrases to avoid**
—**Use of white space**
—**Idea of key execs being time limited**
—**Rewrite as often as required**
—**Check/proof—use of word processors**
   —**spelling (read backwards) spelling checkers**
   —**context: care to avoid context errors**
—**Why are you writing the memo?**
—**Will someone less familiar than you be able to follow?**
—**Being judged on your memos**
—**Never be sarcastic or disparaging**

Figure 11–2. An example of how to document key ideas prior to developing an outline. The ideas documented here formed the nucleus of this chapter.

DEVELOPING THE OUTLINE

Once all ideas are on paper, the next step is to organize them. We favor the use of bubble chart outlines, as suggested by Brogan. Bubble chart outlines are conceptually similar to the outlining method most people learn in high school, but they are much easier to use. The major points are drawn in bubbles on the left side of the sheet (see Figure 11–3, which shows the bubble chart outline for this chapter). Supporting ideas are then extracted from the list of ideas documented in the previous step. These are then added to the major headings on the bubble chart outline in the most logical place. This shows how the ideas fit together, and how they should be organized in the final document.

These supporting ideas are also drawn in bubbles to the right of each major point, and connected by lines to the major points on the left side of the outline. As can be seen in Figure 11–3, bubble charts are easier to use than classic indentured outlines, because ideas can be easily added as the document develops. We have found that bubble chart graphics seem to nurture creativity, make for a more logical flow of ideas, and better show the inter-relationships between different parts of the document. Dotted lines, as shown in Figure 11–3, are used to tie ideas in different parts of the document together.

WRITING THE DOCUMENT

Once the bubble chart outline is finished, writing can begin. If the procedure described above is followed, creating the first draft will be relatively easy. All that needs to be done is to develop the bubble chart ideas into complete sentences, and insert additional thoughts where appropriate.

When following this procedure, it's important to keep several things in mind. Perhaps the most important concept to recognize is that as the writer, you are usually intimately familiar with the concepts being described. You can't make the same assumption about your readers, though. When writing and reviewing the first draft of a business document, you have to ask if the right information is clearly presented, and if it concisely conveys the message. In other words, will someone who is unfamiliar with your work understand the message?

A very common mistake (and a costly one) is to distribute the document as soon as the first draft has been written. We can't over-emphasize the importance of proofreading and rewriting as often as necessary to create a polished and professional document. Whenever possible, give your work a reality check by subjecting it to the over-night test. If schedules permit, set your work aside, and read it the next day. We've often found that 24 hours can make an enormous difference in how one judges one's own writing. If it doesn't read well, rewrite it. Rewriting is much easier than it was a few years ago, now that most companies use word processors instead of typewriters.

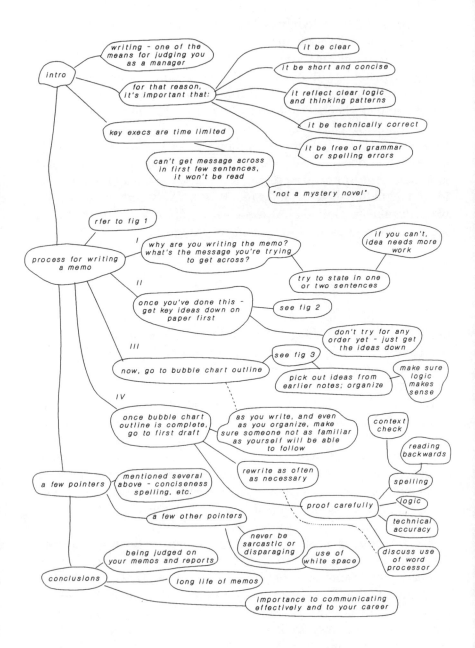

Figure 11–3. The bubble chart outline that preceded the writing of this chapter. Notice how the finished chapter follows this outline.

Spelling can also be easily checked with word processors, as most word processing programs have dictionary features to automatically check for errors. You should recognize, though, that these features won't pick up typographical errors that are misspelled in context, but otherwise correctly spelled. For example, the word "ad" (when you meant to write "at") won't be caught by a word processor's spelling check feature. If your company doesn't use word processors yet, try reading the document backwards. This forces you to look at each word, making typographical and spelling errors more obvious.

We've observed that new managers are occasionally somewhat timid when dealing with secretaries, especially if the secretary does a less than adequate job preparing a memo or other document. Tact and diplomacy (as emphasized elsewhere in this book) are prerequisites to effective management, but don't be afraid to return a poorly typed document to the person who typed it. We require typists to proofread their work before giving it back to us (we've also observed that many secretaries are more than willing to let their bosses do their proofreading). If you encounter this problem, returning a document with typographical errors to the typist *without pointing out the errors* is a quick way to correct it. This forces typists to scrutinize their work more carefully, and reinforces the requirement for careful proofreading. If you allow a document with errors to get out, though, recognize that it's your fault. Blaming it on the secretary at that point (after you've signed the document, or otherwise approved it for release) would be very unprofessional.

After checking the document for spelling and typographical errors, read it through again to see if it makes sense. Are the ideas presented in an orderly and logical fashion? Is the information accurate? Will someone else be able to understand your message, and the logic that supports it? If the answer to any of these questions is no, rewrite the document, and then subject the rewrite to the same questions. If necessary, continue to rewrite. This may seem like a lot of work, but consider the alternative. Remember the question on the opinions we automatically form about authors of poorly written documents? Don't let yourself become one of them. You never know who might read your writing.

A FEW ADDITIONAL POINTERS

This chapter discussed a four-step process for writing effectively, and offered several pointers to maximize the usefulness of this process. The approach outlined in the preceding pages is just a starting point, however. Practice helps quite a bit. There are also several techniques to enhance the quality of one's writing. These techniques include executive summaries, action verbs, professionalism, white space, limiting the use of acronyms, and knowing when not to write.

EXECUTIVE SUMMARIES

We strongly recommend the use of executive summaries. As explained earlier, a good rule is that if you can state the major thrust of your message in one sentence, you have adequately defined it. This one-sentence synopsis can be slightly expanded to form an executive summary, which should be included at the beginning of any business document longer than one page. Everything else will be detailed supporting information, which can follow later.

Executive summaries serve two purposes. They allow readers to quickly digest the message without sifting through the entire document. This is particularly useful for lengthy reports. Executive summaries also entice people to read your writing (everybody loves to see what executives read).

ACTION VERBS

Action verbs make your writing concise, and give it vitality. Simply stated, action verbs, as opposed to passive verbs, show someone or something acting, instead of being acted upon. To understand the difference, consider the following two examples:

He wrote the report.

versus

The report was written by him.

Notice that in the first sentence, the subject of the sentence does something. In the second sentence, the subject of the sentence has something done to it. The first sentence is also shorter than the second, yet it conveys the same message. The style of the first is powerful and direct, while that of the second is weak and passive. We believe this type of writing reads better and we advise using active verbs whenever possible.

PROFESSIONALISM

We can't overemphasize the importance of professionalism in all business writing. Very few people can successfully inject humor into a business memo. Based on the disastrous consequences of a personal attempt at levity, we recommend avoiding it completely. One of us, experiencing a mild level of frustration at a report habitually delinquent from several subordinates, circulated a memorandum instructing the errant staff members that the report was due at 4:15 each Friday. If we had stopped there, we would have had no problems. Unfortunately, we added some remarks that implied those on distribution had difficulty telling time. The memo explained that when Mickey's big hand was on the three and his little hand was just past the four, it was time to turn in the report. Unfortunately, that letter found its way to the company president. By the time it filtered down to our management, we can assure you that the resultant conversation was anything but humorous.

Sarcasm and other disparaging remarks are to be similarly avoided at all times. Not only would such writing be unprofessional, it can also create legal problems for you and your company. As mentioned at the beginning of this chapter, there is a permanence associated with everything you write. A personal attack, in writing, would probably be impossible to defend in court. Even if such a memo did not result in a lawsuit, it almost certainly would cause the boss to question your judgment.

WHITE SPACE

Another technique to enhance your business writing is to use white space. Separate key areas of the report by skipping an extra line or two, and add headings to introduce new concepts. The use of white space makes for easier reading and better comprehension.

ACRONYMS AND ABBREVIATIONS

Almost everyone has endured the experience of reading business letters or reports and stumbling upon an undefined acronym or abbreviation. According to Ralph Slovenko, a professor of law and psychiatry at Wayne State University in Detroit, the use of acronyms and abbreviations often swamps business and technical writing. Unfortunately, acronyms are often confusing to readers who are not intimately familiar with the writer's work. In short memorandums or reports, we recommend avoiding the use of acronyms and abbreviations (there's no need to save space in a short document). In longer reports, acronyms or abbreviations appearing for the first time should be preceded by the expression they represent, as is shown below:

> . . . this information came from the Work Order Request (WOR), and indicates a potential cost overrun. The WOR further shows that. . . .

Subsequent references to the acronym can appear without the expression spelled out, but keep the reader in mind. If the acronym appears again after several pages, there's nothing wrong with spelling it out again. If the report is voluminous and contains many acronyms, consider an index of acronyms and abbreviations at the beginning or end of the report. The idea is to make it easy for the reader to follow your writing.

WHEN NOT TO WRITE

According to Dianna Booher (a consultant specializing in business writing), Americans create 30 billion original documents every year. By any measure, that's an enormous amount of paperwork. Is all of it necessary? Our experience, as well as that of others, tends to indicate that the answer is no.

Several of the techniques previously discussed in this chapter will help reduce the length of business correspondence and reports. The next logical question is: How can one reduce the number of documents?

Booher suggests several ways to do this, including limiting distribution to only those who need to see the document, eliminating unnecessary reports, using outlines to reduce the number of required rewrites, limiting memos to one page, and talking instead of writing.

One technique we've found useful, particularly when moving into new management assignments, is to question the need for every report the organization is required to submit. Our experience shows that one out of every three reports is written to satisfy a requirement that no longer exists (for example, the person who managed the group five years ago wanted the information, higher management wanted the

information on a temporary basis, but the report outlived the requirement, or some other such reason).

CONCLUSIONS

Writing effectively is important because it is a principal means of
communication, and it is one of the key discriminators by which you'll
be evaluated. This chapter presented a process that may appear to be
cumbersome. We believe, however, that the process described here
actually shortens the time required to create a well-written document.
This approach will add professionalism to your writing, and make it
more clear. Effective writing is a very visible skill, and once mastered,
can be an extremely powerful management tool.

Further Reading

Brogan, John A., *Clear Technical Writing*, McGraw-Hill Book Company,
1973.

Otten, Alan L., "Meet Ralph Slovenko, a Professor Who's Also a SOA (Specialist on . . .)," *The Wall Street Journal*, p. 21, August 31, 1987.

Booher, Dianna, "Ten Ways to Cut Paperwork and Do Your Job Better,"
Working Woman, September 1987.

Fielden, John S., "For Better Business Writing," *Harvard Business Review*,
January–February 1965, Number 65103.

Chapter 12
SPEAKING

Mike Aarons listened intently as the conversation unfolded between Mr. Seibert (the bank president) and Tom O'Donnell (one of Mike's peers, a first-level manager in charge of construction loans). Mike, as usual, was impressed by Tom's ability to carry his end of a conversation with a senior executive. Tom always had what appeared to be instantaneous, yet well thought out, answers. The conversation between Tom and Mr. Seibert concerned the relative risks of a significant loan to a small construction company.

"We've never loaned more than a half-million dollars to an outfit that small, Tom. I'm just not sure we can afford to expose this kind of capital, especially with such a small potatoes outfit. What's in it for us?"

Tom O'Donnell answered without hesitation. "Mr. Seibert, it's true that Casler Construction is small, but they've been in the business for eight years, doing mostly residential work. They've managed to show a profit in each of those years, even in the lean times back in the early '80's, when everyone else in residential construction was taking a bath. They're now venturing into commercial construction, and they need new lines of credit. Casler is willing to pay a premium to get it, too, because they know they're largely unknown in that area.

"If we get on board with Casler," Tom continued, "and they do as well in the commercial end of the business as they did in residential construction, we stand to do quite well. We'll get a better-than-average rate of return on the loan, and we'll be available to Casler, as well as other residential construction companies, for other projects. As you know, residential construction lending has been pretty well dominated by First Federal, and we haven't been able to penetrate that market. We have an opportunity to kill several birds with one stone, and we can do it making a better-than-average return on our investment."

Mike marvelled at how well Tom communicated, especially in an impromptu conversation with the bank's chief executive. It always seemed as if Tom knew just what questions would be asked, and always had the right answers.

"Mike, what do you think?" Mr. Seibert asked, turning to Aarons.

Mike Aarons managed the credit research department, a small group responsible for assessing commercial loan applicants' credit history and ability to pay. He had done the work on Casler Construction himself, but Mr. Seibert's question caught him off guard.

"Think, sir? About what?" Mike answered.

Mr. Seibert looked at Mike with a blank stare. "About Casler Construction, obviously. What we've been talking about for the last ten minutes. Their credit history."

When Mike still did not answer, Mr. Seibert asked, "What's Casler's credit history?"

"I'm not sure, Mr. Seibert," Mike said, feeling deeply embarrassed by his inability to answer.

Seibert turned and left. Mike suddenly realized that he did, in fact, know a great deal about Casler's credit history, and it was quite good. He turned to explain this to Tom, but Tom had left, too.

***

In the last chapter, the importance of writing as a means of effective communication was discussed. Speaking is another principal means of communication, and in order to communicate well, being able to speak effectively is as important as being able to write effectively.

The previous chapter also pointed out that writing is one of the principal means by which you will be evaluated. Our experience (and the example above) show that the same holds true for speaking. Poor sentence structure, profanity, mumbling, failure to keep up with the conversation, or any of the other symptoms indicative of an inability to clearly communicate can greatly impede effective management.

This chapter will focus on both extemporaneous speaking and formal presentations. The two require different approaches, but they have several things in common. Perhaps the most significant similarity between extemporaneous and formal speaking is the impact each has on how others perceive you. Another significant similarity is that extemporaneous and formal speaking each contain a bit of the other. Usually, even formal presentations require a fair amount of extemporaneous speaking, simply because you can't anticipate every question you're likely to be asked. Similarly, extemporaneous speaking demands a fair amount of mental discipline and concept development prior to actually speaking. Since extemporaneous speaking is the more commonly used form of speech, let's begin with this subject.

EXTEMPORANEOUS SPEAKING

In order to be a good extemporaneous speaker, you must first be a good listener and a good preparer. That means you have to follow the conversation closely enough to think ahead, determine the direction the conversation is taking, anticipate likely questions, and mentally prepare answers to these questions before they are asked.

This concept was demonstrated in the conversation between Tom O'Donnell, Mike Aarons, and Mr. Seibert. In that conversation, the subject was closely related to Mike Aarons' area of responsibility. If he had paid attention to the discussion (even though he was not yet a participant), it should not have been too difficult for him to think ahead and anticipate where the conversation was going.

Many times, managers find themselves in just such situations. Conversations develop, but if one is not a direct participant, the tendency to allow one's thoughts to drift can become overpowering. One of the key requirements for successful extemporaneous speaking is to track the conversation closely. If the conversation might touch on something you're responsible for, think about what you could add, and consider your responses to potential questions. Jotting a few notes down to guide your answers to more complex potential questions is also a good idea. Doing so assures that your contributions to the discussion and your answers to most questions will be more meaningful. Think of the reaction others will have (and the opinions they will form of you) if your inputs are pertinent, and if you respond to impromptu questions with logical, well thought out answers.

This approach has other advantages, too. Anticipating questions forces one to become more involved in meetings and conversations (it encourages better listening). The practice of anticipating questions also develops the ability to think critically. This enhances the ability to identify potential problems and risk areas.

No matter how good one becomes at this, though, unanticipated questions often develop. When this happens, consider the question carefully before answering it. We've observed that new managers frequently feel a need to answer questions immediately. That can be a serious mistake. Don't be afraid to take a few seconds to organize your thoughts before responding to an unanticipated question. You may even want to respond by saying "let me think about that for a second." If you don't understand the question, say so and wait for clarification before attempting to answer it. Sometimes it helps to repeat the question in order to assure understanding (this also gives you more time to formulate an answer).

The temptation to answer a question immediately can be a strong one, especially if the question is asked by a superior. We've all felt this pressure. It probably occurs as the result of a desire not to appear stupid or slow. If you are afraid to take the time to organize your thoughts or to clarify a question before blurting out an answer, put yourself in the position of the person who asked the question. What do you think would be more annoying—a fast but incorrect answer or an attempt to fully understand the question in order to provide a better answer? The answer is obvious.

While on this subject, one other pitfall bears mentioning, and that's failing to answer the question that has been asked. Discussions with senior managers (and our own experience) show this to be a common and particularly annoying tendency. As a new manager, you've probably already experienced this problem with subordinates. Answers to even simple questions are sometimes so long-winded (and so unrelated to the original question) that by the time the subordinate has given an answer, you've forgotten what you asked. The classic analogy is asking what time it is, and getting instructions to build a wristwatch. Fortunately, there is an effective technique to counter this problem. Ask the person to repeat your original question, and then to answer it. We have found that when this is done, the subordinate usually gets the message, and begins to focus on answering the question that you asked.

Before leaving the subject of extemporaneous speaking, one additional area needs to be addressed. That's when the boss asks to meet with you to discuss a particular topic. We have found that all too often, even when the invitation is extended days or weeks in advance, people show up for such meetings totally unprepared. One mid-level manager at a consumer products manufacturing company told a story that illustrates the problem:

"I expect my first-level supervisors to identify and solve problems. If a problem persists, I assume it's because the supervisor needs help from me. We were experiencing what I suspected might be such a problem in the inspection group, which is managed by a fairly new supervisor. This group is responsible for assuring that incoming materials meet quality requirements.

"As I perceived the problem, there was a severe inspection backlog that threatened to interrupt the flow of raw materials and stop the production line. I asked the supervisor to stop by my office in the morning to talk about the backlog. I expected him to be well prepared to discuss the issues and tell me what he needed to solve the problem.

"When he showed up, though, he was nearly totally unprepared. He didn't know what was causing the problem (although he admitted its existence), and he hadn't thought at all about potential solutions. He basically expected me to solve the problem for him.

"I suppose he thought I invited him to my office for a casual conversation, almost as if we were going to discuss the weather, or a baseball game. That's not the way it's supposed to work. . . ."

The point this story makes is that when the boss wants to talk about business issues, it's not intended to be a social meeting. Usually, the boss will state the subject to be discussed at the time the invitation is extended (if the subject isn't mentioned, don't be afraid to ask). You are not expected to show up at the meeting and then ask, "Okay, what would you like to talk about?" When you have an invitation such as the one described here, recognize that you have an opportunity to become an expert on the subject, formulate and organize your thoughts, and dazzle the boss. You probably won't be expected to give a formal presentation, and you may even want to appear as if you're speaking completely extemporaneously. Nonetheless, when you speak at such a meeting, you should be anything but unprepared.

FORMAL PRESENTATIONS

Formal presentations are those that are planned in advance, designed to cover specific topics, and often involve the use of visual aids (such as presentation charts, films, or demonstration hardware). Formal presentations may be internal management reviews, training sessions, or marketing presentations to current or potential customers. Whatever the case, the objective of a formal presentation is to clearly communicate the message in a polished and professional manner. Preparation for a formal presentation should include planning, research, outlining, assembling the rough and formal drafts, and rehearsing.

PLANNING

Like any other activity requiring the integration of many tasks, successful formal presentations require good planning. Most of these tasks are described below, but recognize that each tasks contains numerous subtasks, all of which must be completed prior to the presentation. For example, preparing the formal draft of the presentation charts will require artwork, secretarial support, proofreading, and corrections. In order to assure adequate time is allotted for each of these subtasks, a good plan is essential. (Additional information on good planning practices can be found in Chapter 1.)

RESEARCH

You should become as knowledgeable as possible in the area your presentation will cover. We recommend gathering all pertinent information, forming preliminary conclusions, and then discussing these conclusions with others who might be affected by what you present. This approach will allow you to learn of most objections or disagreements with the material you plan to present. If the objections are valid, it may be necessary to modify the recommendations or conclusions you intend to present. If you choose not to do so, simply being aware of potential areas of disagreement will facilitate a better presentation. Prior discussions may disarm most of the criticism you might otherwise hear during the presentation. If the areas of disagreement cannot be resolved prior to the presentation, though, at least others in the audience will realize the material has been coordinated with all who might be affected.

OUTLINING THE PRESENTATION

Once the research phase is complete, the information should be outlined in exactly the same manner as described in the previous chapter on writing. Put all thoughts on paper, and then prepare a bubble outline. After completion of the bubble outline, preparing the presentation charts will be much easier than writing the first draft of a narrative document. That's because presentation charts use brief descriptions to convey your message (this will be covered in more detail shortly), and most of the statements already in the bubble outline won't need to be expanded.

PREPARING THE ROUGH DRAFT

The use of presentation charts is strongly recommended for formal presentations. The material you present will have much more of an impact and will be better remembered if the people you present it to both *see* and *hear* the information.

We have also found that the best format for such charts involves the use of bullet statements. Bullet statements are terse, topical descriptions that are covered in more detail during the presentation (an example of this format is shown in Figure 12-1). According to Lee Iacocca, formal presentations are more effective when the material is organized into three sections, as described below:

Introduction. The introduction gives an overview of the major topics included in the presentation.

Body. In the body of the presentation, the subject material is communicated to the audience.

Summary. In the summary, briefly review the material you presented. In many cases, the summary chart will be identical to the introduction chart (except that it will be titled "summary" instead of "introduction").

We, too, have found this three-step approach (tell them what you are going to tell them, tell them, and tell them what you told them) to be quite effective. It is widely used in many types of formal presentations. The introduction entices your audience to pay attention, the body of the presentation delivers the main message, and the summary wraps it all up.

There are a few additional points to consider when preparing the presentation charts. One is to get the major thrust of your message across using as few words as possible. Don't use complete sentences, and don't be excessively wordy. (Note the way this is done in Figure 12-1.) If your charts are too wordy, you'll find that the audience will be reading the charts when they should be listening to you. Use the words on the charts to support what you say, and deliver most of the message verbally. The chart is intended to reinforce what you say, not to duplicate it.

Limit the number of concepts introduced on each chart to no more than three. If you think more are necessary, pick out the most important three, discard the others, and see if your message still makes sense. If you want to cover more than three points for each major concept, you can either use a continuation chart, or better yet, cover the additional points verbally. Showing more than three points on each chart will make the chart too wordy, resulting in the same problem discussed above (people will read the charts instead of listening to you).

Wherever possible, use graphs and illustrations. These make it easier to explain more complex concepts. If you work in a manufacturing company, you may even want to use demonstration models or actual hardware to make your points. This is particularly useful in sales presentations, but the technique also enhances internal presentations,

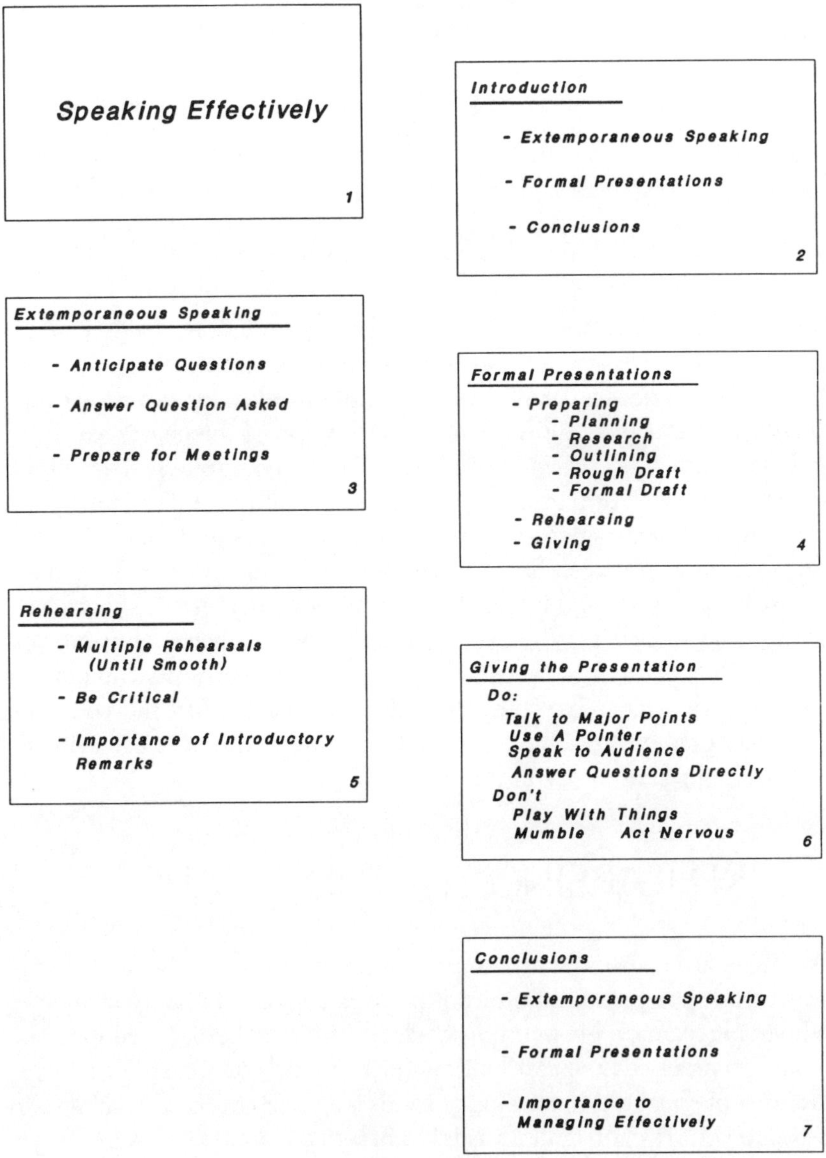

Figure 12-1. Formal presentation charts for a presentation on speaking effectively. Note the organization, the use of bullet statements, and the limit of no more than three major concepts per chart. In the presentation, the speaker should verbally cover most of the information, using the major points listed on the charts to reinforce the presentation.

especially those given to senior executives. Senior executives enjoy seeing the product, because it makes your message much more readily understood, and it gives them a chance to handle the hardware, which they don't get to do very often. Using the product as part of the presentation also strengthens your credibility (by showing that you are close to and familiar with the product).

PREPARING THE FORMAL CHARTS

Once the rough draft is complete, the presentation charts can be typed, or, if necessary, prepared with larger graphics. Larger letters are sometimes necessary in bigger meetings to allow for easier reading. Make sure your plan allows enough time to proof the charts carefully and have any necessary corrections made. Typographical or other errors will be very apparent during the presentation, and can hurt your credibility. During sales presentations, such errors hint that the product or service you are offering may not meet very high quality standards. In both sales and internal presentations, such errors show a lack of attention to detail. When reviewing the formal charts, check to see that the flow of ideas is logical. If the order of the concepts you plan to introduce doesn't make sense, reorder the charts until the concepts flow smoothly, with each one logically leading to the next. Be critical, because your audience will be.

REHEARSING THE PRESENTATION

Once you are satisfied with the presentation materials, the next step is to rehearse the presentation as often as necessary. The importance of rehearsing cannot be overemphasized. Find an empty conference room and practice the presentation until you feel comfortable with it. If the idea of speaking to an empty room is disturbing, find someone to listen to you. It's not at all unusual to practice a presentation five or six times until it sounds right. Doing this allows you to move more smoothly from one chart to the next, and to memorize the key points you want to make on each chart.

During the rehearsal, be critical. Anticipate questions to the information you present, and formulate answers to these questions. If you identify questions that cast major doubts on the validity of the presentation, reconsider your material. If the material is wrong, finding out and correcting it now is better than having someone else point the problem out during the presentation.

Spend a good deal of time getting the first minute or so of the presentation perfect (even to the point of committing the exact words to memory). This portion of the presentation should be the smoothest and best delivered part. As Joe Girard, one of the world's most successful salesmen, says "Get them with you from the start and they'll stay with you." The impression you make at the beginning of the presentation will probably be the one the audience leaves with, so you want it to be as favorable as possible.

GIVING THE PRESENTATION

On the day of the presentation, go to the conference room early enough to make sure everything is perfect. See if the projector works and is properly focused (you don't want to have to adjust it at the beginning of the presentation). Check to make sure enough chairs are available. Make sure the room is comfortably air-conditioned or heated. Your goals should be perfection, because if there are any distractions, both you and the message you want to deliver will be communicated in a less effective manner.

When you give the actual presentation, don't be afraid. It's perfectly natural to be nervous, but don't let this natural nervousness compromise your presentation. Take that nervous energy and put it to work for you. Be enthusiastic about the material you present, but speak slowly and clearly. Most people have a tendency to speak faster in a formal presentation, so make a conscious effort to guard against doing this. When questions are asked, use the same techniques discussed earlier in this chapter to answer them.

Speak directly to your audience, maintaining good eye contact with the people you are speaking to. In addition to involving the audience, this can also help to reduce speaker nervousness. Don't talk to the presentation charts, as this will quickly cause an audience to lose interest. Don't play with the change in your pockets, the pointer, or anything else. Be enthusiastic, and your audience will take more interest in what you have to say.

By the time you give the presentation (assuming you've done your homework), you should be an expert on the material. Don't forget that, because it will bolster your confidence, and confident speakers are more readily accepted by their audiences.

CONCLUSIONS

In this chapter, both extemporaneous speaking and formal presentations were discussed. Good extemporaneous speaking occurs in response to anticipated questions. If responses to these potential questions are developed as the conversation progresses, your extemporaneous speaking skills will improve sharply.

Formal presentations require much more preparation. Like extemporaneous speaking, though, formal presentations require anticipating likely questions. Rehearsing is an important part of preparing for formal presentations, because it polishes your speaking and adds professionalism to the presentation. Mastering the skill of speaking effectively, whether done extemporaneously or as part of a formal presentation, is a critically important management skill.

Further Reading

Girard, Joe, *How to Sell Anything to Anybody*, Simon and Schuster, 1977.

Iacocca, Lee, *Iacocca—An Autobiography*, Bantam Books, 1984.

Halsey, William D., *Macmillan Contemporary Dictionary*, Macmillan Publishing Company, Inc., 1979.

Bashor, Pamela H., and Hankins, Marion, "Keep Talking," *Sky*, Halsey Publishing Company, July 1987.

Connelly, J. Campbell, *A Manager's Guide to Speaking and Listening*, American Management Association, 1967.

Chapter 13

CAREER PLANNING

Most managers do not attain their positions by chance. Becoming a manager and continuing to rise through the management ranks occurs as a result of careful career planning. Many managers, and those who want to become managers, aspire to positions of greater responsibility, and, as is frequently the case when attempting complex objectives, detailed planning is required. Planning your career requires planning skills very similar to those discussed in Chapter 1. Career planning is an important part of career management, and career plans (like all other plans) require establishing both objectives and a means of achieving the objectives.

DEFINITIONS OF SUCCESS

If a career plan is to be effective, it must begin with an objective. When asked about career objectives, most managers would probably answer by saying they want to be successful. This leads to a very abstract question, though. What constitutes success?

Success has greatly varying definitions, depending upon one's personal aspirations, values, self-image, background, credentials, age, and a host of other factors. We took an informal poll of the managers we work with and asked them to define career success. Here's a sampling of the answers:

Getting on the bonus plan
Being able to fly first class
Getting the job done
Making $100,000 per year
Being respected by fellow workers
Continuing career advancement
Being promoted to regional sales manager
Being promoted to director
Being promoted to vice president
Becoming president of the company

As can be seen from the above answers, definitions of success vary widely. Interestingly, managers who defined success as attaining higher level positions had answers that fell into two categories. One group defined success as a promotion to the next management level (i.e., one step above their current positions), while the other group defined success as a management position several levels higher than their current positions. This is a significant distinction, as will be explained later. For now, let's recognize that success is a personally defined concept, and one person's definition can be greatly different than another's.

CAREER OBJECTIVES

In order to plan your career, then, you need to have an idea of what constitutes career success. Our experience indicates that most new managers define career success as continuing advancement in one form or another, with the measure of success being increasing responsibility and compensation. Our view is supported by more formalized management research. D. Levinson, for example, found that career growth is the dominant objective for younger managers. Levinson's research also shows career progression is less important to most managers beyond age 40 (Levinson found that after 40, family and other activities take precedence over career advancement). Recognizing that career objectives can change, however, does not diminish the significance of defining career objectives and building plans to support them.

An important first step in career planning (as in any other form of planning) is to define your career objectives. Do you want to be president of the company? Do you want to be the senior executive in your field of expertise (for example, the vice president of marketing, or the vice president of engineering)? Would you be happier as a middle manager in one area (perhaps regional sales director)? Perhaps you do not aspire to more senior management positions, but would prefer technical specialization instead. As described in Chapter 6, many high-technology companies provide dual career paths; one in management, and the other in areas of technical specialization.

Whatever the choice, it must be yours. Only you will spend the better part of a career pursuing it, and only you will know if you are happy when (and if) you get there. Helping to define your objectives is beyond the scope of this book.

However, we will make one recommendation about the process of defining career objectives. Take the long term perspective, and focus on objectives you would like to achieve 15 to 20 years downstream (or further). Planning of any type (including career planning) is more effective if it looks at the big picture. This inherently makes sense. If you focus on a promotion one step above your current position (and are successful in attaining it), will the new position posture you for further success? You run a serious risk of accepting a dead-end promotion if you focus on only short-term gains, and don't take the long view.

CHANGING NEEDS

Evolving personal needs (and how they change as a function of age) were discussed earlier. In planning your career, you may want to take these probable changes in personal aspirations into account. It's also important to recognize that as one progresses through the management ranks, the skills required at each level in the organization change.

R. L. Katz describes these shifts in skill requirements as changing positional needs, and further explains that they can be segregated into three categories, which are in turn based on three levels of management. First-level managers must have good technical skills (like those of their subordinates), but the need for those skills is eclipsed by needs for administrative, planning, and motivational skills. First-level managers and supervisors obviously need to be technically astute, but more importantly, they need to be able to plan the work, assure that adequate resources are available, and motivate their subordinates to perform well.

The second level Katz describes is middle management. The skills needed here emphasize strength in political and interpersonal relationships. Middle managers must be able to forge alliances within their organizations to facilitate accomplishing work objectives. The manager of the marketing function, for example, must be able to work closely with the manager of the manufacturing function so the company sells as much as it can manufacture, but doesn't commit to more than it can produce.

Top management makes up the third level. The skill requirements here focus on conceptualizing and strategizing. This inherently makes sense. Company presidents, for example, would be ineffective chief executives if they focused on micro-managing individual departments. The top management of a business organization should instead focus on strategic decisions, and providing company-wide business direction.

Another model developed by the Aerojet General Corporation graphically shows how management skill needs both evolve and overlap through different management levels (this model is shown in Figure 13–1). In this model, the skill requirements discussed by Katz are condensed into three categories: technical, interpersonal, and strate-

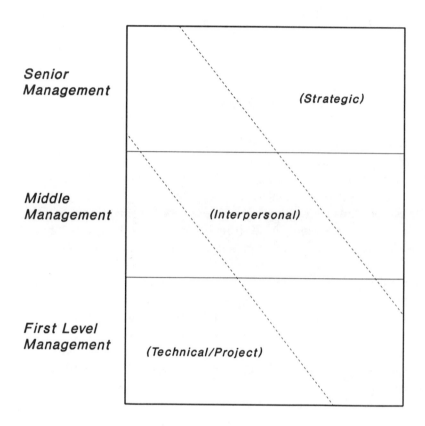

Senior
Management

(Strategic)

Middle
Management

(Interpersonal)

First Level
Management

(Technical/Project)

Figure 13–1. A model showing management skill needs as a function of level in the organization.

gic. This model shows that each of the three management levels (first-level, middle, and senior management) require all three skills, but the emphasis at each level is different.

The purpose of this discussion is not to make you an expert on different management skill models, but rather, to instill an awareness of the evolving nature of skills requirements as one progresses through the managerial ranks. Stated differently, the skills that work well for a first-level manager probably won't work well in a middle management position. When considering your career objectives, this should be taken into account. Do you have the skills necessary to be successful in higher level positions? If you don't, can you develop these skills? What is necessary in order to do this? The answer to the last question, in particular, will provide many of the interim milestones of your career plan.

ESSENTIAL INGREDIENTS

The discussion above focused on the changing needs of different levels of management. There are a few constant needs, however, that might be called essential ingredients for continuing career success. These essential ingredients are independent of management level. Many of them have been mentioned elsewhere in this book, but bear review here because of their significance.

Probably the most important requirement for any manager is the ability to get along with others. In our opinion, no one expresses this requirement better than Lee Iacocca, chairman of the Chrysler Corporation. Iacocca regards an inability to get along with others as a kiss of death. As he explains it, the reason is humorously simple. Chrysler doesn't hire dogs, monkeys, or other animals; they only hire people.

Another essential ingredient for management success is the ability to motivate people in a manner that creates an inner desire to do the job well. There are many ways to motivate people, but the trick to doing this successfully on a long-term basis is to create an environment in which the desire to do the job well comes from within. Our experience has shown that while negative incentives can be made to work for short periods, they don't work well on a long-term basis. People forced to perform in an environment of constant negative incentives ultimately leave their organizations for less threatening environments. Positive incentives can motivate people for longer periods (particularly financial incentives), but they do not provide a long-term solution, either. Most companies relying exclusively on financial incentives ultimately become non-competitive. There is no simple answer to the challenge of motivating people, but most management research suggests that identifying individual motivations, and then providing an environment in which these motivations can be satisfied is the most successful approach.

One of the prominent theories of motivation maintains that people are motivated by three needs: a need for achievement, a need for affiliation, and a need for power. A corollary to this theory holds that management style depends to a great extent on which of these three needs are dominant. Research indicates that more successful managers have approximately equal achievement and power needs, with lower needs for affiliation (as illustrated in Figure 13–2). In the context of this research, a need for power is not considered to be a negative attribute (i.e., a need to dominate others), but can instead be described as a need to influence others. This profile makes sense, as it seems reasonable

that successful managers would be both achievement-oriented and
adept at influencing others, yet are not overly concerned with a need
for affiliation.

The point is that you may want to consider your motivational needs.
We're not suggesting that you change them if they differ from the
profile described above for most managers. After all, your management
style got you to your current position. You should be aware, though,
that a considerable body of research indicates most successful managers are motivated by needs for influence and achievement.

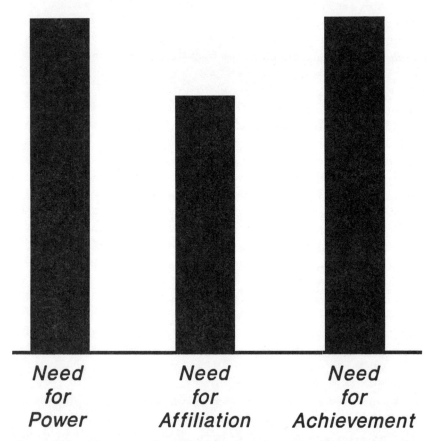

*Figure 13–2. Motivational needs profile for most successful managers. The
needs for power and achievement are high and approximately equal, with
the need for affiliation somewhat lower.*

Another essential requirement for management success is the ability
to control one's emotions (and in particular, to refrain from showing
negative emotion). Name-calling, threats, and derogatory remarks are
all displays of negative emotion, and are to be carefully avoided. Think

about how you would feel (or have felt) as the recipient of such a display. Subordinates (at all levels) expect more professional behavior from their superiors. Managers who disappoint their subordinates by violating this requirement are demotivating, and are generally considered to be non-promotable by their superiors.

Successful managers also accept responsibility for the shortcomings of their subordinates. This is perhaps best exemplified in the military services. Military officers are taught to accept responsibility for everything their organizations achieve or fail to achieve. Our experience has shown that with only slight modification, this concept also applies to the business environment. The rule is simple. If your group does poorly, *you* take the blame. If they do well, *they* get the credit. The reasons for this are straightforward. If the organization you manage fails to meet a commitment, you are responsible, and you should take the criticism. Attempting to justify your performance by blaming the failure on a subordinate is extremely unprofessional. Your superiors, peers, and subordinates will almost certainly develop a very low opinion of you. Most middle and upper managers know what's going on in their organizations, and they realize that many of the shortcomings are not directly attributable to the first-level manager. By attempting to pass the blame to your subordinates, however, you are telling the boss that you won't accept responsibility. You are also telling your subordinates you won't take the heat if they make mistakes. Few people would want to work for such a person.

On the other hand, if a subordinate makes a mistake and you accept responsibility (i.e., you don't attempt to defend yourself by blaming your subordinates), you also send a powerful message. Under these circumstances, most subordinates will realize you are on their side, and that you all form a team. Many subordinates (in our experience) are highly motivated if they see the boss attempting to help (rather than condemn) their efforts.

Just the opposite holds true for praise. Don't accept it personally. If your boss (or anyone else) compliments your performance, tell that person the good results are due entirely to the people who work for you. Both your subordinates and those offering the praise will hold you in high regard.

COMPANY REQUIREMENTS

Some of the general requirements for management success were described above. These should be examined in light of the successful management styles in your organization. Most companies (and often sub-organizations within companies) have their own prerequisites for management success. Analyzing these requirements can be tricky (it's a safe bet they won't be written down anywhere). Nonetheless, your company's profiles for success can be assessed, and we have found that intelligent applications of the results can be quite beneficial.

Perhaps the best place to begin is with the motivational profile discussed in Figure 13–2. You might attempt to reconstruct this chart for your company. For example, if the president of the company and most of the senior managers spend considerable time developing personal relationships with their peers and subordinates, a strong need for affiliation may be a prerequisite for success in your company. Caution in such an analysis is required, though, as the development of personal relationships might also be an attempt to influence others (thereby indicating a need for power).

Companies often have more easily identified educational profiles. This is particularly true for sub-organizations within the company. It almost goes without saying that an engineering degree is a prerequisite for success in an engineering organization, and that a business or accounting degree is a requirement in a financial organization. You might look into the other academic credentials of the managers in these organizations, though. Do most of the managers have MBAs, or other advanced degrees? Does any one school seem to predominate? When David S. Lewis was chairman of the board at General Dynamics, for example, graduates of the Georgia Institute of Technology seemed to advance more rapidly than others (Lewis is a Georgia Tech graduate). Similarly, graduates of the California Institute of Technology have done well at Aerojet General (Theodore von Karmann, who started Aerojet General, also had a hand in the formation of Cal Tech).

With a little thought, other patterns for success are also discernible. In many manufacturing companies, for example, production management experience is a prerequisite for advancement. In retail sales organizations, marketing or accounting experience often provides an advantage. Look at the top people in your company, and find out what kind of assignments they had on the way up.

Presentation and decision-making styles also provide a good gauge of the prerequisites for advancement. When faced with important decisions, do the senior managers in your company tend to prefer quantitative analysis, or do they instead prefer subjective judgments? Are presentations carefully staged affairs, or are informal meetings more the norm? All of these discriminators provide clues that can be used to your advantage.

MANAGING THE BOSS

So far most of this book has focused on managing downward (i.e., managing your subordinates). Managing up (or managing the boss) is equally as important (not only to help your organization achieve its objectives, but also to help you realize your career objectives). We'll illustrate this with a story about a friend of ours who used this technique to realize considerable career growth.

Charlie was a brand manager in a consumer products company. Shortly after he joined the company, it experienced a major reorganization, and Charlie found himself reporting to a new boss. The two had diametrically opposed management styles. The boss was gruff, seldom followed through on anything, managed through intimidation, and generally made emotional, snap decisions. Charlie liked to lead by example, and preferred a systematic, analytical approach to decision-making. The boss was about 25 years older than Charlie, and had a production background. Charlie came from a marketing environment. Most people thought the reporting relationship wouldn't work out, and for about six months, it didn't. Charlie was thoroughly disgusted, and soon initiated a job search.

After about six months, though, things started to get better. About two years later, the two were still working together, and Charlie had been promoted twice. He ultimately became the boss's most trusted subordinate. We were more than intrigued with this transformation, and we asked Charlie how it came about. His answer was as intriguing as the change in the two men's relationship:

"I was ready to quit. I wanted to quit. I didn't think I could stand another day of his abuse. Then one day I told the story to a friend of mine who works at another company. He listened to me, and then said 'Look, you can leave a good job, or you can learn to manage this guy . . . just because he's the boss doesn't mean you can't figure out what makes him tick, and use that to manage him. . . .

"I thought about that, and then, more out of curiosity than anything else, I set out to see if I could do it. I studied that guy, and I learned everything I could about him—his style, his positive aspects, his negative aspects, everything. Instead of getting mad when he did something I didn't like, I filed it away, for future reference. I learned about the way he stands there and rubs his arm when he's unsure about something. I learned how to recognize when he's under stress. I learned his likes and his dislikes, and what his weaknesses were. I saw, for example, that he often gave out assignments and then didn't bother to follow through on them, but that he needed someone to follow through, and get the information to him.

"I started by giving him the results of the assignments he handed out, both to me and to others. Then I realized he didn't like to plan, so I started doing that for him, in my area as well as others.

"I think that was the key. In short, I made myself indispensable to him, without ever asking or telling him that's what I was doing. It's paid off very well. . . ."

The reason we tell this story is that it's one of the most dramatic examples of managing the boss we've ever seen, and it contains many valuable teaching points.

For one thing, Charlie's experience shows that it's not necessary to like the boss (or have the boss like you) in order to be successful. You may not agree with the boss all of the time (or even most of the time). You may not like all of the boss's traits. If you do not focus on these dislikes, however, and instead focus on analyzing the boss's likes, dislikes, motivations, weaknesses, and other idiosyncrasies, you can then adapt to them. Once you adapt to them, you are effectively managing the boss.

When analyzing the boss, there are several factors to consider. One is how well he or she likes to be kept informed. Some bosses want to know everything, and make all the decisions. Others only want to know about major problems, and rely heavily on their subordinates to make decisions. You may not like it if your boss fits into the first category, but you will be a good deal happier if you recognize and adapt to it.

Another factor is how the boss makes decisions. Some bosses prefer a great deal of quantitative analysis prior to making decisions. Others like to make subjective "gut-feel" decisions (with little supporting information). A sure clue to a boss who fits in the first category is if he or she continually asks for more information. Bosses in the second category can be recognized by their tendency to avoid reading reports or studying background information. These bosses, when confronted with difficult decisions, often turn to their subordinates and say "tell me what to do." If you work for this kind of boss, you'll be miles ahead if you know how to answer this question, and have the background material ready to support your recommendation.

Bosses also vary in their preference for verbal versus written communications. Some bosses like to be told of important developments, while others prefer the message to be documented in a letter. Still others like to be told and given a letter (to back up the message, or perhaps to serve as a reminder). Look at how others communicate with your boss, and use the methods that are successful in getting the message across.

Identifying the boss's weakness is particularly helpful, because if you can help the boss in these areas, you will become a highly valued subordinate. This is also an area, however, in which caution and diplomacy are required. You don't want to say, for example, "Look, I know you're not too sharp in this area, so maybe I can help. . . ." As our friend Charlie did, offer your help in a nonthreatening manner. The boss will realize what you're doing, and appreciate it all the more if it's done with subtlety.

Two additional topics to consider are the boss's dislikes and priorities. Obviously, it makes good sense to avoid those things that upset the boss. You may feel, for example, that attending professional seminars is a worthwhile thing to do. If the boss thinks such meetings are a waste of time, however, it would probably be unwise to spend company money to attend an expensive, time-consuming out-of-state seminar. Similarly, find out what the boss places a high priority on, and focus your effort on those projects. This must be done with caution and balance, however. You should be aware of the critical success factors of your position, and make sure all bases are adequately covered. In other words, you can't ignore the rest of your job and focus only on those things important to the boss. Avoid the boss's dislikes, emphasize those things the boss likes, and focus your efforts on those projects the boss prioritizes.

HANDLING SETBACKS

No discussion on career management would be complete without addressing career setbacks. All careers have ups and downs. The positive factors can be exhilarating. Promotions, raises, increases in responsibility, major sales, and the simple satisfaction of doing a job well are all rewarding experiences. Unfortunately, career setbacks can evoke negative feelings that are just as powerful. Being passed over for promotions, being demoted, not getting a raise, or losing a job are major disappointments. Surveys indicate, however, that at least one or more of these setbacks occur in most people's careers.

How we deal with these setbacks is critically important not only to how others perceive us, but to how we feel about ourselves. If you're denied a promotion and force a confrontation with the boss, he or she will probably be convinced they were correct in giving the job to someone else. If you brood about not getting the promotion, you compound the problem by making yourself miserable. The same holds true for most other career setbacks.

We've found that when faced with setbacks, the best way to react is by being nonemotional and objective. Evaluate the factors behind the setback. If you lost a promotion, was it because the other person was more qualified? If you lost your job, was it due to factors beyond your control? If the boss gives you a smaller raise than you expected, did your performance truly merit a larger increase? If, after an objective assessment, you conclude you have been treated unfairly, you are faced with a decision. You can tough it out, continue to do excellent work, and wait for the situation to change. Or, you can look for another job.

SHOULD YOU LOOK FOR ANOTHER JOB?

According to Hitt (a management specialist with the Battelle Institute), most people who change jobs voluntarily do so because of a perceived lack of opportunity for growth inside the company. The key word is perceived, and that ties in to the discussion above on maintaining objectivity when faced with career setbacks.

Perhaps the most significant issues to face when making a decision to look for a new job are how much you enjoy your current job, and how well your current job tracks with your career plan. Does your plan call for you to be further along than you are now? Are you simply disappointed in not getting a promotion or a raise you feel you deserve? If it appears that you are falling behind where you planned to be, is your career plan still realistic? All of these are important questions, and all are designed to help you determine if your current job is what you really want to do.

If you're disappointed with where you are in the organization, and after objective self-evaluation you feel the situation is improper, we recommend talking to your boss about it. Above all else, be diplomatic, and don't threaten to quit. Ask the boss what his or her plans are for you, and explain your career objectives. If the two don't track, ask what you can do to change the situation. You should realize going in to such a meeting that most bosses will feel uncomfortable, and unfortunately, not all bosses will answer these questions honestly. Only you can be the judge of your boss's answers.

If you conclude that the best course of action is to seek employment elsewhere, take your time, and keep your job search confidential. We recommend not telling anyone in your company. Even close friends can inadvertently leak information. No matter how upset you've become with your current management, don't quit before you've found the job you want (it's much more difficult to find a job if you're unemployed). Don't take the first job you're offered just to escape. It's very tempting to accept the first offer, but don't do it until you're satisfied the new job tracks with your career objectives.

CONCLUSIONS

This chapter covered several critical aspects of career management. Developing your definition of success is an important first step in formulating a career plan. This helps to define long term objectives, and increases the probability of happiness while pursuing these objectives. As managers mature, personal needs change. So do positional requirements as one advances through the managerial ranks. While the requirements of different management positions change, there are several essential ingredients to management success that are independent of management level. Some of these ingredients are constants, while others are peculiar to specific organizations. Managing the boss is a crucial requirement for management success, as is the ability to handle setbacks in an objective and non-emotional manner. The final subject considered in this chapter was looking for another job, and the decision criteria to consider when making this choice. All of these factors are critical elements of career management, but perhaps none are as important as the first step—developing a personal definition of success.

Further Reading

D. Levinson cited in R. F. Pearse and B. P. Pelzer, *Self-Directed Change for the Mid-Career Manager*, American Management Association, 1975.

R. L. Katz, "Skills of an Effective Administrator," *Harvard Business Review*, September-October 1974.

Maslow, A. H., "A Theory of Human Motivation," *Psychological Review*, Vol. 50, No. 4, July 1943.

McClelland, D. C., "Comments on Professor Maslow's Paper," *Nebraska Symposium on Motivation, III*, University of Nebraska Press, 1955.

McClelland, D. C., "The Two Faces of Power," *Journal of International Affairs*, Vol. 24, No. 1, 1970.

McClelland, D. C., and Burnham, D. H., "Power Is the Great Motivator," *Harvard Business Review*, March-April 1976.

Hitt, William D., *Management in Action*, Battelle Press, 1985.

Bolles, Richard Nelson, *What Color Is Your Parachute?*, Ten Speed Press, 1984.

Hegarty, Christopher, *How to Manage Your Boss*, Ballantine Books, 1985.

Iacocca, Lee, *Iacocca—An Autobiography*, Bantam Books, 1984.

Part IV

GLOBAL TASKS

Chapter 14
MEETINGS

Keith Henderson looked at his watch. It said 2:37. It was two minutes since the last time he checked. The meeting was long, boring, and apparently without purpose.

Keith was annoyed. He managed the art department at a construction management company, and had been invited to the meeting to offer his ideas on the layout and graphics of a new proposal for a medium-sized shopping center. At least that's why Keith *thought* he had been invited. Two minutes into the meeting it became quite clear that the person who called it, Paul Laurenz (the project manager), had no idea what the proposal strategy would be. Paul wasn't even attempting to solicit help from the attendees. The conversation seemed to go in circles, with no conclusions being reached. It was apparent to Keith that no one in the meeting was attempting to move the discussion in any direction.

After another three minutes, Keith looked at his watch, and decided he had enough. He got up and quietly moved towards the door.

"Well, I guess we're done," Paul said.

Keith felt embarrassed for a second, and mistakenly thought that Paul had taken offense at his rising to leave and was being sarcastic. Keith was surprised to see that Paul was serious, as he and the others also got up to leave.

"These meetings really are a waste of time," Paul said to no one in particular. Keith was even more surprised. Paul had called the meeting.

***

An inescapable fact of management life is that managers spend significant portions of their time in meetings. We've had days in which virtually 100 percent of our time was spent in meetings, from the time we walked in the door, through a "working lunch," until the time we went home. Our experience shows that on any given day, most managers spend between 25 and 50 percent of their time in meetings. No matter how the statistics are interpreted, that's a significant portion of anyone's time.

Many of these meetings are a necessary aspect of management life, as they provide a means to accomplish several functions. Communications of all types (including both giving and receiving information), problem solving, planning, decision-making, and a host of other management activities occur in meetings.

The discussion in this chapter will focus on the meetings managers spend most of their time in, meetings that range in size from three or four people up to those with fifteen to twenty people. Larger assemblages are not really meetings as defined in the context of this chapter. (Such meetings tend to be presentations to audiences, with greatly reduced two-way dialogue between the speaker and those in the audience.) Chance encounters or other impromptu meetings, such as dropping in on a colleague to seek his or her advice, will also be excluded here. The intent of this chapter is to focus on maximizing the effectiveness of those meetings in which most of us spend our time, and what actions are required in order to do this. Specifically, four areas will be covered:

- activities occurring before meetings,
- activities occurring during meetings,
- activities occurring after meetings, and
- how to eliminate unnecessary meetings.

Proper attention to each of these areas will maximize the efficiency of meetings, and eliminate those which do little other than consume valuable time.

ACTIVITIES OCCURRING BEFORE MEETINGS

The first thing to consider when calling a meeting is whether the meeting is necessary, and what you hope to accomplish as a result of the meeting. As mentioned earlier, a variety of management activities occur in meetings. One of the steps in preparing for a meeting is deciding which of these activities should be accomplished at the meeting. These activities generally fall into four categories:

Information Giving. Managers disseminate information in these meetings. Examples include regularly scheduled staff meetings (in which the manager relays information passed down by his or her boss), special meetings to establish ground rules at the outset of new projects, presentations, and any other meetings in which information is provided to others.

Information Collecting. These meetings are called to allow managers (or anyone else who calls the meeting) to collect information prior to making a decision. Examples include meetings to gather quarterly sales figures, accident investigations, or other meetings in which the principal purpose is to gather information.

Problem Solving. In these meetings, the participants define problems, identify their causes, and select the best solutions (problem solving will be covered in more detail in Chapter 15).

Decision-Making. These meetings are quite similar to problem solving meetings, but the outcome is focused on arriving at a decision.

Although four categories of meeting activities are presented here, we're not suggesting that the purpose of a meeting must be restricted to only one of these categories. In practice, meetings are often a blend of at least two or more of the above categories. A meeting may have as its purpose disseminating information, gathering any related information from the other participants, and making decisions based on this information. We suggest that prior to calling any meeting, you carefully decide what you want to accomplish in the meeting, and then structure the meeting along the lines of one or more of the categories described above in order to accomplish your objective. When making this decision, make sure the meeting is really necessary. You owe it to yourself (as well as to others) to eliminate unnecessary meetings, and to make those that are necessary as productive as possible.

Once you've defined the purpose of the meeting, the next step is to prepare an agenda. Agendas are critically important to the success of a meeting. They give succinct statements concerning the purpose and topics to be covered, and thereby provide a road map for the conduct of the meeting. This gives the meeting's participants a sense of direction and a vehicle for organizing their contributions.

We recommend that the agenda include five elements: a title, the time and place, the purpose, a list of topics to be covered, and who is invited to the meeting (a sample agenda is shown in Figure 14–1). When listing the agenda topics, it's a good idea to list the names of those expected to be the principal sources of information next to each topic. This alerts the people you invite to be prepared.

There are several factors to consider when determining the time and place for the meeting. Our experience shows that meetings usually should not last longer than one hour. When meetings run longer than this, they usually lose effectiveness rapidly. The participants often become bored and restless and begin to think about other things. A good trick to keep meetings from running too long is to schedule them to end when some other activity is scheduled to begin (such as lunch, quitting time, or another meeting). This tends to keep the meeting moving. Another technique that works particularly well for shorter meetings (those lasting only ten or fifteen minutes) is to remove the chairs from the meeting room. Stand-up meetings seldom last longer than scheduled.

In addition to being time-efficient, meetings should also be timely. It wouldn't make sense, for example, to meet about the loss of a major account if the event occurred over a year ago. Similarly, it would be unwise to postpone a meeting about an impending important event. Meetings must be closely linked to the information, problems, and decisions they address.

Common courtesy dictates that meetings be located closest to the center of mass of the participants. For example, if your meeting requires participation from people who work at two different facilities, the meeting should be held at the facility where most of the meeting participants are located. Two exceptions are meetings with the customer and meetings with senior executives. These should be held at locations that are convenient to the senior people or customer participants (unless, of course, these people want to hold the meeting at another location).

The next issue is to determine whom should be invited. Two factors are involved here. In order to limit the size of the meeting, you should invite only those people who are absolutely necessary to the meeting. On the other hand, you don't want to offend anyone who might feel left out or purposely excluded if they are not invited. The approach we've used is to invite those who must attend (to provide essential information, make key decisions, etc.), and then offer optional invitations to others who might be interested. A good format for doing this is shown in the sample agenda of Figure 14–1.

As an aside, if someone else has called a meeting you feel a need to attend but you haven't been invited, don't hesitate to ask for permission to attend. We've never seen anyone deny permission when faced with such a request. Another approach is to simply go to the meeting as if you had been invited. Under such circumstances, we've never seen anyone asked to leave, either.

The last thing to do prior to the meeting is to prepare for it. We recommend bringing copies of the agenda for everyone. Do this even if you've distributed the agendas prior to the meeting, because many invitees don't bring their agendas with them. Make sure the conference room is ready, and has everything you and the other participants might need (such as an overhead projector in good working order, coffee, etc.). It's also a good idea to contact the key participants before the meeting to make sure they're prepared. Tell them how important their inputs are to the success of the meeting, and what they need to bring with them (such as the results of analyses, sales figures, new product concepts, etc.). Sometimes it helps to invite the key participants' bosses. If the participants see that their bosses have been invited, they are more likely to be prepared.

One last comment is in order. Be on time. There are few things as annoying (or rude) as managers who are late to their own meetings.

AGENDA

Northwest Marketing Strategy Meeting
Executive Conference Room, Building 2
3:30 to 4:30, October 14

Purpose: To establish preliminary concepts for pricing and distribution for the next fiscal year.

Topics to be addressed:
1. Current problem areas (Simmons)
2. Competitor pricing practices (Jones)
3. Competitor distribution practices (McClain)
4. Recommended pricing strategies (Edwards)
5. Recommended distribution strategies (Ortega)

Invitees:

Simmons	Ortega
Jones	Johnson (optional attendance)
McClain	O'Leary (optional attendance)
Edwards	Corleone (optional attendance)

Figure 14–1. An example of a meeting agenda. Note that it contains five elements: title, time and place, purpose, list of topics, and an invitation list.

ACTIVITIES OCCURRING DURING MEETINGS

The activities required to prepare for meetings were discussed above. Once these have been completed, the stage is set for an effective meeting. The manner in which meetings are conducted, however, is equally important.

We recommend beginning the meeting by briefly reviewing the agenda. Everyone's thoughts will be focused if you state the purpose of the meeting, review the agenda items to be covered, and mention how long the meeting should last. If it's likely that action items will be assigned during the meeting, ask someone to serve as a recorder.

Once the meeting is underway, it's also a good idea to summarize the key thoughts and decisions that emerge as the conversation progresses. This tends to keep the meeting moving, as it helps to prevent the discussion from drifting back to topics already covered. It also gives others an opportunity to disagree if your perceptions are incorrect.

Controlling the meeting is important to assuring its success. You don't want to be overbearing, but you don't want to let the meeting become a waste of time, either. Controlling the meeting doesn't mean that you have to dominate the conversation. It does mean, however, that you have to guide the participants in following the agenda and achieving the meeting's objectives. Be an alert listener, and give others the opportunity to develop their thoughts. If the conversation drifts too far from the published agenda, let it continue for awhile. Most of the time, someone else will speak up to get things back on track. If this doesn't happen, interrupt politely at a convenient break and recommend a return to the agenda. A simple statement like "We're getting a little off the subject, and we only have this room for an hour . . ." usually works very well.

Another consideration involves controlling sub-meetings within the meeting. This is especially true if the meeting has more than five or six participants. It's not at all unusual for two or three people to start talking among themselves, apart from the conversation involved in the main meeting. If this is allowed to go on for more than a brief period, you may find that two or three smaller meetings are in progress, and most of the room is no longer concentrating on the speaker, or the issues on the agenda. At this point, speaking up is essential in order to get the meeting under control. One executive we know handles this situation particularly well by raising his hand and loudly proclaiming "Let's have one meeting. . . ."

We've all experienced the situation in which one individual dominates a meeting. It's difficult to overcome this problem in a nonoffensive manner, but we've found that simply asking others for their opinions tends to quiet a domineering participant. For example, a statement like "those are good thoughts, Ed . . . now, John, what do you think?" is quite effective.

Insults are more difficult to handle. Our experience shows that the best way to handle an overt insult is to simply ignore it. Offering a counter-insult is childish, and tends to lessen your control of the meeting. Surprises are more subtle insults, and like all management activities, are best handled in a nonemotional manner. Ask the person with the surprise information why the issue wasn't brought to your attention earlier. This both neutralizes the intended insult and alerts others in the meeting as to the true intent of the surprise. Here's an example that shows how effective this can be:

In a corporate sales meeting, several marketing executives were discussing quarterly sales figures from the organization's numerous marketing districts. A female executive had particularly low sales figures in one of the five sales districts she managed. When the conversation in the meeting focused on this district, she began to explain the reasons for the unexpectedly low performance. Before getting very far, however, one of the other executives interrupted. He surprised everyone by saying that if the district sales manager didn't drink so much, the district would have probably done better. The group was embarrassedly silent for a few seconds, until the regional manager spoke up. "I didn't realize he had a drinking problem," she said. "How long have you known about this, and why didn't you tell me about it sooner?" Needless to say, the executive who made the derogatory comment fell silent.

The last pitfall to watch for in conducting a meeting is a hidden agenda carried in by one or more of the participants. In this situation, the carriers of the hidden agenda want to accomplish something other than the stated purpose of the meeting. If your meeting starts to follow a hidden agenda, use the same tactic discussed above for keeping the meeting on track. Explain that the meeting is drifting from its intended purpose. Sometimes a suggestion to convene a subsequent meeting to address the purpose of the hidden agenda is also effective.

Budget your time in the meeting, and don't dwell too long on one agenda topic to the exclusion of the others. At the close of the meeting, you should summarize the discussion, state the main points or decisions, and review the action items. At this point, it's a good idea to ask for action item completion dates. People usually feel compelled (particularly when asked in front of others) to commit to completion dates, and then to meet those commitments.

ACTIVITIES OCCURRING AFTER MEETINGS

If you've done your homework before the meeting, and effectively managed the meeting, your activities after the meeting will be both straightforward and brief. We recommend publishing the action items (along with the people assigned and the completion dates) within 24 hours. This not only serves as a reminder, but when issued promptly, helps to convey a sense of urgency about the assignments.

Recording the key decisions and issuing minutes of the meeting also helps to solidify the results. We've found, however, that this is usually necessary only for the more formal meetings (such as meetings between companies or with major customers). For internal meetings, issuing meeting minutes is not as important. Published action item assignments, however, are important.

Once the action item assignments and, if necessary, minutes of the meeting have been issued, the final step is following up to make sure the assignments are completed. The people to whom action items are assigned may not report to you. Seeing each person individually to determine the status of their response is probably not a good idea—the assignees may resent you checking up on them. We've found the best way to handle this is with a follow-up meeting, which specifically focuses on the assigned action items. In our experience, the participants of such follow-up meetings generally accept the necessity of the meeting, and come prepared.

ELIMINATING MEETINGS

The beginning of this chapter mentioned the amount of time most managers spend in meetings. Obviously, cutting back on the number of meetings you attend would allow more time for other management tasks. Eliminating unnecessary meetings, then, is a very worthwhile objective. There are several ways to do this, as explained below.

Log All Meetings. Many meetings are redundant, and could be combined with a little bit of forethought. By keeping a log of recent meetings and reviewing those scheduled in the near future, you may find meetings similar enough to be combined.

Avoid Calling Meetings. As discussed earlier, you owe it to yourself (as well as others) to only call a meeting if it is absolutely necessary. If you can state a clear purpose for a meeting, and you need it to facilitate attaining your organization's work objectives, then by all means conduct the meeting. If the objectives can be met more expeditiously by other means (such as one or two phone calls), then don't call a meeting.

Avoid Committees. While committees offer certain advantages discussed elsewhere in this book (such as visibility, networking, etc.), they are also a seemingly unending source of meetings. If you need to join committees (for whatever reason), recognize that by so doing you are probably committing yourself to additional meetings. If you can avoid serving on committees, you will cut back on the number of meetings you'll be asked to attend.

Question Invitations. Don't go to meetings simply because you've been invited. Ask yourself if you are really needed, and if the answer is no, ask the same question to whoever is calling the meeting. Explain that you don't feel a need to be there, and ask to be excused. If the other person is adamant about your attendance, see if you can send a subordinate to sit in for you.

The above are merely suggestions, but our experience has shown that they can substantially reduce the number of meetings a manager has to attend. These suggestions, when combined with the other techniques described in this chapter, generally make the remaining meetings one must attend far more productive.

CONCLUSIONS

Attending meetings is an important part of any manager's job. Meetings occupy a good deal of management time, so managers owe it to themselves (and others) to maximize the efficiency and effectiveness of meetings. This can be accomplished with intelligent planning and organization before, during, and after meetings, and by eliminating unnecessary meetings. As explained earlier, the activities that go on prior to meetings are particularly important. Most meetings that fail do so because they were unnecessary to begin with, or because they were poorly planned or managed, or because they had inadequate follow-up. The thoughts offered in this chapter are designed (and have been successful for us) for overcoming each of these problems.

Further Reading

Verderber, Rudolph and Kathleen, *Inter-Act*, Wadsworth Publishing Company, 1980.

Ranftl, Robert F., *R & D Productivity*, Hughes Aircraft Company, 1978.

Jay, Antony, "How to Run an Effective Meeting," *Harvard Business Review*, March-April 1976.

Chapter 15

PROBLEM SOLVING

One of the things that makes managing so demanding is what at times seems like a never-ending stream of problems. Problems can be a source of frustration and anxiety, but consider this question: Isn't solving problems one of the key things that managers get paid to do? We believe the answer to this question is yes. Simply stated, solving problems is a big part of the management job.

The most successful approach we've found for solving problems consists of a four-step process that answers four questions.

Question 1. What is the problem?
On the surface, this appears to be an easy question to answer. It seems obvious that this question should be addressed before proceeding with the search for solutions. Unfortunately, this doesn't always occur. More often than not, managers attempt to find a solution before the problem has been identified. We'll show how easy this is to do by working through an example. And if the real problem hasn't been identified, any attempted solution has a very low probability of success.

Question 2. What is the cause of the problem?
In order for an auto mechanic to fix an engine that doesn't run, he must first discover what's wrong with it. The same concept applies to solving management problems. Once the problem has been identified, you have to discover its cause. Problems and causes are often confused, and this frequently confounds implementation of an effective solution.

Question 3. What are the solutions?
Almost all problems have more than one solution. It's important to identify all of these solutions, along with the advantages and disadvantages of each. Managers need to be option thinkers and avoid the tendency to grasp at the first solution to come along.

Question 4. What is the best solution?
Once all potential solutions have been identified (along with the advantages and disadvantages of each), the last step is to select and implement the best solution.

The four-step problem-solving process occurs naturally after using it for a while. If you're not used to approaching problems this way, though, the process can take some getting used to. Our experience indicates that this adjustment process occurs very quickly, and for more managers, the process rapidly becomes a preferred and automatic way to approach and solve problems.

In all too many cases, however, the problem-solving process described here isn't used. The outcome is predictable when this occurs. The real problem remains unresolved, and creates other problems that are frequently more serious than the original problem.

A PROBLEM OF DECLINING SALES

Sharon manages a sales group in a distribution company that sells electronic components to computer manufacturers. The computer industry has been experiencing a recession, and sales are generally down. In particular, sales to one customer have recently declined significantly. One of Sharon's junior sales representatives recently closed a major sale with this customer, but the outcome was disappointing. Both the quantity of components ordered by the customer and the price per unit were lower than what Sharon had expected. Sharon had counted on the sale to make her quarterly sales projection. The size and low dollar amount meant she would miss this commitment.

Based on the sales representative's description of the negotiations, it also appeared that relations with the customer are deteriorating. Sharon knows she has a problem, but at this point, she's not sure what the problem is, or how to go about fixing it.

Question 1. What is the problem?

Is it that the order was too low? Did this occur because the industry is depressed, and it's the best Sharon could expect under the circumstances? Were Sharon's prices too high? Does the sales representative have a personality conflict with the customer, or did he simply do a poor job? Did Sharon make a mistake by sending a junior person to handle a critical customer? Is missing the sales projection the real problem?

Determining the problem is the most difficult part of the problem-solving process. We've found that the best way to do this is to examine each issue that might be a problem, and ask if the issue causes something to occur, or is the *result* of something else that has occurred. This difference is subtle, yet significant. Examining each issue raised above will solidify an understanding of this process.

Was the order too low? The low order caused something else to occur (the missed sales projection). We can therefore dismiss the size of the order as not being the problem.

Is it due to a depressed market? Similarly, the depressed market caused something else to occur (the low order, and the missed sales projection). This issue can also be dismissed as not being the real problem.

Were Sharon's prices too high? The high prices probably caused the low order and the missed sales projection. The price is not the basic problem, either.

Was there a personality conflict? At this point, Sharon doesn't have enough information to answer this question. Let's move on to the next issue.

Did the sales representative simply do a poor job? Again, Sharon doesn't have enough information yet to answer this question.

Was the sales representative inexperienced? Like the two preceding questions, inadequate information is available to answer this question. More research may have to be done to answer these questions.

Is missing the sales quota the problem? Unlike all of the other potential problems listed above, this is the only issue that occurs as a *result* of the others.

Even though Sharon doesn't have enough information to answer all of the questions described above, she does have enough to recognize the basic problem. She will miss her sales quota. Everything else is an influencing factor, and are issues to be concerned about. But Sharon's underlying problem is that she will miss the sales quota.

Question 2. What is the cause of the problem?

As is typical in most management situations, Sharon doesn't have as much information as she'd like to. Her attempts to identify the problem have provided some good insights into several potential causes, but Sharon wants more information before deciding upon the major causes. After talking to the sales representative and the customer, she learned that even though the recent negotiations were heated, neither the sales representative nor the customer appear to bear any animosity towards the other. The customer mentioned something else, however, that is significant. Sharon's prices were much higher than those of her competitors. The customer told Sharon that because of her high prices, the customer's management had directed placing the majority of the order elsewhere.

With this information, Sharon now had a feel for the dominant cause of the problem. Her prices were too high.

Question 3. What are the potential solutions?

One obvious solution is to lower the price. Sharon wants to consider the advantages and disadvantages of each option, though. Lowering the price will reduce profit per unit, but it should also increase the number of units sold. The increased sales may offset the lowered profit per unit. Sharon could also leave her prices high, or perhaps even raise them, and settle for a higher profit margin on lower quantities of components. Discussions with her customer and recent experience, however, indicate that this will cut deeply into sales. Further discussions with Sharon's finance and purchasing department indicate that she could lower the prices and still sell at a profit.

Question 4. What is the best solution?

Based on Sharon's identification of the problem, its cause, and the potential solutions, Sharon made a decision to lower prices.

CONCLUSIONS

We've discussed a four-step problem-solving method that consists of identifying the problem, the causes of the problem, all potential solutions, and the best solution. This technique is extremely effective. It can be used to solve problems at every level in the organization. We did not develop this technique. It was taught to us by the president of a billion dollar company, who learned it as a college student more than 40 years ago. Our experience indicates that most successful managers use this approach, and when they present their ideas in this problem-solving format (problem, cause, potential solutions, and best solution), the logic of the approach tends to sell the recommended solution.

Further Reading

Hitt, William D., *Management in Action*, Battelle Press, 1985.

Leavitt, Harold J., *Managerial Psychology*, The University of Chicago Press, 1978.

Interview with E. R. Elko, President, Aerojet Ordnance Company.

Chapter 16
USING CONSULTANTS

Consultants are frequently maligned through jokes and misunderstandings about what they do, but if used effectively, consultants can be very powerful management tools. The degree to which consultants are used in most organizations varies widely. Some managers feel consultants are a panacea for all problems. Other managers avoid consultants like the plague.

One prominent management consultant (Holtz) has two humorous descriptions that offer an insight into why some managers hesitate to use consultants. The first maintains that a consultant is anyone who is out of work and owns a briefcase. The second portrays a consultant as someone who borrows your watch to tell you what time it is.

Considerable confusion often surrounds the definition of a consultant, and that's probably where most of the jokes and negative feelings emanate from. Let's begin our discussion by attempting to define what a consultant is.

WHAT IS A CONSULTANT?

The dictionary defines the term *consult* as ". . . to refer to for information or advice . . .," and further defines a *consultant* as ". . . one who gives professional or technical advice. . . ." These definitions put us in the ballpark, but for our purposes a more specific set of definitions is required. These will address the two categories of temporary help most people have in mind when they refer to consultants.

The first category is the independent consultant or team of consultants. These people are typically expert in a specialized area. There are numerous areas of specialization, a few of which will be discussed shortly. Such consultants are usually independent business entities, and work on a contract basis. Typically, the independent consultant is called in to solve a specific problem. Larger consulting firms may send several individuals to solve more complex problems, but the distinguishing feature of this type of consultant is that the purpose of the consulting engagement is to solve a specific problem.

The other type of consultant is a specialist that performs temporary contract labor. Like the first category of consultants, these people may be hired individually or in teams. Unlike the first category of consultants, though, the temporary contract laborer is not usually retained to solve a specific problem. Instead, these consultant often do the same kind of work as full-time employees.

Consultants in this category are usually full-time employees of contract labor firms that specialize in providing temporary help. This help can be in any of several areas—accounting, engineering, sales, clerical, etc. Most often, such contract labor is brought in to help companies during periods of peak demand, or to provide temporary help during a period of business growth (until the company can hire enough full-time employees). Contracted temporary helpers often accept full-time employment at the companies where they are consulting. Such an arrangement is used by many companies, as it provides an opportunity to more thoroughly evaluate a person's work before extending an offer of employment.

The biggest difference between the two categories of consultants is that the first type of consultant specializes in solving specific problems (and developing the solution to the problem generally concludes the consulting engagement). Consultants in the second category generally do the same kind of work as full-time employees of the company at which they are consulting. Consultants in the first category usually work under their own direction (once the problem to be solved has been agreed upon by the consultant and the client), while contract labor consultants take day-to-day direction in the same manner as full-time employees. This difference can have important legal ramifications (as will be explained later), and is one reason consultants in the second category are usually full-time employees of contract labor companies.

AREAS OF SPECIALIZATION

Consultants are available in practically every field. In the marketing area, for example, there are advertising consultants, promotion consultants, distribution consultants, pricing consultants, competitor intelligence consultants, consumer preference consultants, and hundreds of others. Management consultants can specialize in organizational design, organizational development, attitude surveys, compensation, finance, union negotiations, and many other areas. In the scientific and technical communities, the list of available consulting specialties is endless. There are design consultants, statistics consultants, warranty consultants, aerodynamic consultants, computer programming consultants, and many, many more. In short, almost anywhere a need for specialized skills exists, consultants may be found. Finding the right consultant can be a challenge, but the first decision the manager usually faces is determining whether a consultant is needed.

WHEN DO YOU NEED A CONSULTANT?

Bringing in a consultant is not a decision to be taken lightly. Consultants are not cheap, and if the need for one is not real, both your company and you can suffer. Usually, consultants are retained for one of three reasons. Two of these reasons are tied to the type of consultant, while the third reason is related to an entirely different consideration.

The first reason to retain a consultant is to solve a problem that cannot be solved with the skills available within your organization. If your group is facing a problem it cannot solve (or is having difficulty defining the problem), bringing in outside help may be the wisest course of action. This has ramifications, though, which must be considered before a consultant is retained. If the problem is one your group ought to be able to solve but cannot, bringing in a consultant may be perceived as a threat by some of the people in your organization. You need to consider if the problems this perceived threat could cause are worth the expediency of consultant assistance. On the other hand, if no one in your organization specializes in the area in which you need assistance, consultant help will probably be welcomed by all within the group.

For example, suppose you manage a sales group in a retail store that is converting to price-code bar charts to provide point-of-purchase price reading by optical character sensing devices. Bringing in a consultant to instruct your group on likely customer reactions and how best to deal with them would probably be well-received. On the other hand, if your group is responsible for designing merchandise displays and you retain a consultant to solve a problem in this area, you may encounter some resistance from others who might feel their jobs are threatened.

The second reason for retaining consultants involves an overload situation. Overload situations can be brought on by seasonal increases in work requirements, a hiring rate that cannot keep pace with business growth, or other specific business needs. For example, consumer-oriented companies that manufacture items for discretionary purchase frequently contract with temporary agencies for help during the Christmas holiday season. Similarly, a defense firm that wins a large contract may need temporary engineering, manufacturing, or quality assurance help until it can hire the people it needs.

The third reason for retaining a consultant involves an entirely different consideration. This is when a third party is needed for reasons of objectivity, or to propose a distasteful solution. For example, suppose a company's top management wants to determine if it is being paid appropriately. For reasons of objectivity, the president of the company would probably not want to ask the vice-president of personnel to make this determination. The vice-president of personnel, as a direct report to the president, would probably be inclined to recommend an increase in salary. A consultant specializing in compensation for chief executives could be more objective (although an article in *The Wall Street Journal* concluded that even a consultant would be reluctant to recommend anything but a pay increase; that is, if the consultant looks forward to future business with the same client).

The other situation involves the use of a consultant to propose a distasteful solution, one to which the manager hiring the consultant does not wish to be tied. Suppose you are attempting to solve a problem, and it's apparent to you that the ideal solution calls for a reorganization that would decrease another manager's responsibilities. If you bring in a consultant to solve the problem and the consultant arrives at the same conclusion you did, the other manager will probably be upset, but at least the recommendation for reorganization didn't come from you. An added advantage is that such a recommendation may be better accepted by other managers from a neutral third party.

A closely related decision to the question of retaining a consultant is how long the consultant should be kept on the payroll. If you retain temporary contract labor consultants, the answer is simple. Temporary help of this type should be kept on as long as is necessary to get the job done (in other words, until the period of peak demand is over, or until enough permanent employees are hired to meet the company's increased personnel needs).

The length of time for consultants brought in to solve special problems, though, will depend on the nature of the task. Our experience tends to indicate that most consultant engagements are for less than one year and nearly 50 percent are for less than six months, with the majority of consulting assignments being measured in weeks rather than months.

HOW TO LOCATE A CONSULTANT

Once you've made a decision to call in consultant help, the next challenge is locating the proper consultant. To a large extent, this task will depend primarily on the type of consultant you need. If you need temporary help, for instance, your organization's personnel department will probably be familiar with the local temporary agencies. If the personnel department in your company does not have this information, the yellow pages are a good place to start (look under employment-temporary, engineers-consultant, and other similar headings).

The help wanted advertisements in local newspapers (especially the Sunday editions) also frequently carry ads by temporary employment services. Although the intent of these ads is to *hire* temporary help (for placement elsewhere), the advertisements are a good way to get to know the agencies in your area. If you can't find an agency that offers the kind of temporary help you are searching for, most are usually willing to provide referrals. Placement officers in temporary agencies are anxious to be of assistance. The temporary agency may not have people with the skills you currently require, but they will want you to remember them when you have a future need.

Locating the first category of consultant described earlier (i.e., the independent problem-solving specialist) is usually more difficult, but there are several ways to approach this problem. The easiest is to consider consultants that you or someone else in your company has used before to solve similar problems. If this approach doesn't prove fruitful, call other consultants who have worked for your company and ask for referrals. Consultants often maintain extensive contacts with each other, and are very willing to refer colleagues. If other consultants cannot provide a referral, try calling your colleagues in other companies, particularly those whose work is similar to yours.

Another approach to locating an independent consultant is to contact professional societies or use symposia proceedings. Awareness of such societies and symposia is a good idea for other reasons, too, as was explained in the chapter on career planning. The local chamber of commerce may have a registry of local consultants. One last approach is to contact people who have retired from your company and are specialists in the area in which you need help. Such individuals are often willing to return as consultants for short-term assignments, and offer the added advantages of familiarity with the company, its product line or services, and the problems you face.

HOW TO EVALUATE A CONSULTANT

In many ways, evaluating a consultant prior to signing a contract is similar to hiring a full-time employee. This is particularly true for consultants who provide temporary contract help (i.e., consultants called in to do the same kind of work as full-time employees). In fact, every temporary agency we've dealt with sends prospective temporary helpers to interview with the client company prior to placement.

In many other ways, however, hiring a consultant is much different from hiring a full-time employee. This is particularly true for the independent problem solvers. For both categories of consultants, it's prudent to check references. Remember the anecdote at the beginning of this chapter about a consultant being anyone who is out of work and owns a briefcase. Unfortunately, there are quite a few individuals who fit this description and call themselves consultants. You don't want to find that out after you bring the consultant into your company, so get a few references and check them out.

When interviewing a prospective consultant and checking with his or her references, you should search for several qualities that characterize successful consultants. The first (and perhaps most obvious) is technical expertise. The consultant must be proficient in his or her area of specialization, and must be able to solve the problems or do the kind of temporary work you have available. Evidence of professional competence may be obtained through conversations with previous clients, by reviewing papers or other documents the consultant has published, and by interviewing.

A few words are in order about interviewing consultants, particularly those who are independent problem solvers. You will probably want to discuss the assignment with the consultant and assess his or her answers. Be aware of the fact that consultants are in business to sell advice, however, and probably won't solve the problem for you during the interview (if consultants did that, you wouldn't need to hire them). Assessing a consultant in this situation requires a careful evaluation of the answers to your questions. A good consultant should be able to quickly outline an approach to solve the problem, without necessarily providing the solution. You need to be wary of consultants, though, who have never worked the type of problem you face but are willing to give it a try. Unfortunately, some consultants are more than happy to take on assignments in which they have no particular expertise.

Other desirable consultant attributes include confidence, an ability to rapidly come up to speed, and the ability to listen. Obviously, a consultant must radiate confidence. You don't want to bring in an expert to solve a problem who is unsure of his or her capabilities.

Similarly, consultants must be able to quickly grasp the essence of a problem, and rapidly converge on the best solution. You can't afford the luxury of a lengthy training period. This is partly due to the rates consultants charge (which will be discussed later), and partly to the politics of retaining a consultant. Consultants get high visibility in most organizations, and if the consultant's performance is anything less than exemplary, it can reflect negatively on you.

Finally, the consultant must have the ability to listen. If the consultant repeatedly cuts you off during the initial interview, chances are the consultant is a poor listener. We've found the best consultants tend to ask a few key questions that indicate a fundamental understanding of the problem, rather than simply making many statements and asking numerous questions in an attempt to impress the interviewer.

We can't overemphasize the importance of assessing the consultant's listening abilities. The danger in retaining a consultant who doesn't listen is that he or she may not fully understand the problem you want solved or the issues you face. When this happens, the consultant can spend considerable time solving the wrong problem, and that translates into wasted budget. We've seen this happen frequently in the aerospace industry, with poor results all around: The customer was displeased, the managers who retained the consultants fared poorly on their performance appraisals, the consultants lost the client companies as customers, and the problems went unsolved. A senior aerospace industry manager once humorously referred to a hard-working consultant who solved the wrong problem as a person with "high terminal velocity, but little guidance and control. . . ."

CONSULTANT RATES

The next issue is establishing a fair price for the consultant's services. In most cases, there will be very little, if any, negotiation. Good consultants have established rates and a list of clients who are happy to pay them. Usually the consultant states his or her rate, and you are faced with a take-it-or-leave-it situation. As explained by Michael E. Porter (*Competitive Strategy*, The Free Press, 1980), if the consultant can save the company time or money, most companies are fairly insensitive to price.

Consultant rates frequently appear to be significantly higher than those paid to full-time employees doing similar work, and this often causes consternation to new managers or others retaining consultants for the first time. As the manager hiring the consultant, you should understand some of the factors that influence their rates. Consultants are balancing the security of steady employment against the uncertainty of consulting engagements. While a full-time employee knows where the paycheck is coming from each week, the consultant frequently does not. Additionally, consultants must spend a sizeable portion of their time marketing (i.e., searching for new consulting engagements). Consultants are often more specialized than full-time employees, and this also influences their rates. Finally, consultants do not enjoy the same benefits as full-time employees, such as medical and dental plans, tuition-reimbursement programs, and insurance (to name but a few). For these reasons, consultants typically bill at rates higher than the wages paid to full-time employees doing similar work.

Our experience indicates that consultants generally charge about double the hourly rate of a full-time employee. For instance, a financial analyst might earn about $40,000 per year, which equals about $20.00 per hour. A consultant in this field, therefore, would probably quote an hourly rate around $40.00 per hour. Similarly, a consultant engineer would probably quote a rate in the vicinity of $50.00 an hour if full-time employees doing similar work were earning about $50,000 per year.

These guidelines are now quite flexible, however. Many consultants will bill below these rates in order to penetrate a market, of if the availability of consulting assignments is low. In times of high demand or in more specialized fields, consultants may charge in excess of $100.00 per hour. It's not unusual for the rates of highly specialized consultants to be over $1,000 per day. Consultants may charge on a daily or a weekly basis, and some charge by the job.

The rates discussed above apply primarily to the first category of consultants (independent problem solvers). Pay for consultants in the second category (temporary help from contract or job shops) is governed by a different set of rules. In this case, the consultant is a full-time employee of the job shop. The job shop typically offers some benefits, although they are usually less than those of their client companies. This allows the contract labor consultant's rate to be lower than the rates discussed above. Unlike the case for the independent consultant, however, the temporary contract worker's job shop keeps a percentage of the contract worker's pay as profit for its services. For that reason, your company will probably end up paying as much (or nearly as much) for a consultant from a job shop as it would for an independent consultant (although the job shop consultant would take home less).

One last factor to consider when assessing a consultant's price is that even though the consultant may be earning more than your full-time employees, it may actually be cheaper to use the consultant. That's because the cost of a full-time employee to the company is considerably more than just his or her salary. The total cost includes benefits, vacation, sick time, office space, and a host of other overhead cost elements. These other elements can be significant. Some companies consider the actual cost of a full-time employee to be two to three times the employee's salary. By comparison, even a relatively high-priced consultant may be inexpensive.

ADVANTAGES OF USING CONSULTANTS

There are many advantages to using consultants. Obviously, a wisely chosen consultant brings special skills to the organization, and allows you to solve problems you might otherwise not be able to. Another advantage is that consultants allow you to smooth out the peaks and valleys in your organization's workload. During busy periods, consultants can help the organization meet all of its requirements. If you couldn't use consultants, you would be left with three relatively distasteful choices—asking people to work excessive overtime, hiring extra-help full-time employees (and probably laying them off when the workload diminished), or not getting all of the work done. The consultants' flexibility allows you to overcome this problem. Consultants, by the very nature of their work, understand that their stay with a company is temporary. In fact, many of the consultants we know resist longer-term assignments, preferring a large number of short-term contracts instead of one or two long-term ones.

We've already discussed the cost and pricing issues associated with retaining consultants. As mentioned previously, even though a consultant may bill at what appears to be a fairly steep rate, the cost to the company may be less than that of a full-time employee.

One final advantage is that consultants are generally more objective than full-time employees. Consultants don't have political turf wars to fight, they're not interested in promotions or raises, and they're not tied in to intra-company networks. For these reasons, it's often easier to accept advice from a consultant than from a full-time employee. This can be helpful, especially if there's a need to propose a potentially unpopular recommendation. The recommendation may be more readily accepted if it comes from the consultant.

DISADVANTAGES OF USING CONSULTANTS

Before concluding this chapter, a review of some of the disadvantages of using consultants is also in order. The most obvious disadvantage is the consultant's generally high billing rate, although as discussed previously, this is more of an imaginary problem than a real one. The real cost danger, however, is if the consultant attempts to solve the wrong problem. In that situation, the cost can be very high.

Another disadvantage is that consultants cannot always be hired on short notice. The better ones tend to have customers waiting in line, and you may not be able to get the consultant you want.

We've also found that some consultants may have an overly-narrow perspective when approaching problems. This can usually be overcome by spending enough time with the consultant at the beginning of the engagement to assure the assignment is well-understood, but even then, the issue of perspective can be a problem. According to Leavitt (a management researcher and author) it's usually because the consultant attempts to apply a previously successful solution to your problem (i. e., the consultant tries to make your problem fit a known solution). Again, appropriate management attention can prevent this from occurring.

For a variety of reasons, consultants are often perceived as a threat by some full-time employees. Obviously, if your group can't solve a problem and you bring in a consultant, some of your people will probably feel threatened. This problem can be overcome with the techniques to be discussed in Chapter 18 on managing conflict. The compensation issue can also be threatening. It's easy for a full-time employee to forget about the benefits he or she enjoys when working alongside a consultant earning what appears to be twice as much (or more). This problem can be circumvented by not disclosing the consultant's billing rate (or if the billing rate becomes known, by explaining the reasons behind it).

Some managers fear a loss of proprietary data when dealing with consultants. Although we've heard of this being raised as an issue numerous times, we've never seen it to be a real problem. Most consultants are acutely aware of the need to preserve a reputation for maintaining client confidentiality. If the company has a real concern about proprietary information, a nondisclosure clause can be written into the consultant's contract (most of the consultant agreements we've seen contain such clauses).

One final disadvantage in using consultants is the potential legal consequences of retaining an independent consultant for an extended period of time. In a few cases, courts have held that such consultants were actually employees of the company, and as such, entitled to all of the benefits normally afforded to full-time employees. The decision criteria appears to be the duration of the consulting engagement, and whether the independent consultant worked with the same kind of day-to-day management direction received by full-time employees. Being considered a full-time employee can be a problem if the consultant suffers an injury or illness during a long-term consulting engagement and sues the client company. If the court declares the consultant to be an employee of the client company (instead of an independent contractor), the client company (and not the client company's insurance carrier) can be financially liable for the consultant's medical expenses. This problem can usually be overcome by requiring the consultant to provide proof of medical and liability insurance prior to the consulting engagement. Because of these and other potential legal entanglements, we strongly recommend that you review all potential consulting agreements with your company's legal department prior to retaining any consultant.

CONCLUSIONS

Consultants can be a very powerful management resource. As discussed in this chapter, consultants exist in every imaginable field. The challenge in obtaining good consultant help is in locating a consultant that specializes in the area in which you need assistance, and then determining if the consultant can do the job. Consultant rates frequently appear to be significantly higher than the wages paid to full-time employees doing similar work, but when other factors are taken into consideration, most consultant rates are justified. There are powerful advantages to be had by using consultants, but there are also disadvantages. Both must be considered in the decision to retain a consultant.

Further Reading

Holtz, Herman, *How to Succeed As An Independent Consultant*, John Wiley and Sons, 1983.

Steiner, George A., Miner, John B., and Gray, Edmund R., *Management Policy and Strategy*, Macmillan Publishing Company, Inc., 1982.

Webber, Ross A., *Management*, Richard D. Irwin, Inc., 1979.

Porter, Michael E., *Competitive Strategy*, The Free Press, 1980.

Leavitt, Harold J., *Managerial Psychology*, The University of Chicago Press, 1978.

Chapter 17
MANAGING CHANGE

"Look, Bob, that's just not going to work around here. We've been doing it this way for twenty years and we haven't had any complaints, so we must be doing something right. We get the job done, and that's what the people we support like."

Bob Taguchi was stunned by the comment and by the reaction of his group. All ten members of the Test Department sat in front of him, stone-faced. Several had their arms crossed, and many were staring at the floor. At least Rod Pinowicz had the courage to speak up, and say what very obviously was on everyone else's mind. Still, Bob couldn't understand why the group was so intransigent.

The problems had started about two months earlier, almost as soon as Bob took over the Test Department. The group was part of a large engineering organization in a defense company, and conducted tests to support product development efforts for the rest of the company. The Test Department enjoyed an excellent reputation for its responsiveness and "can-do" attitude, but it had a serious safety problem. Injuries in the lab were occurring almost every week. The injuries were minor in nature, but Bob feared that a serious accident was inevitable, primarily due to poor experimental design and the group's lack of formal safety training.

To Bob, the answer to the problem was obvious. He felt the Test Department needed to conduct a review prior to each test, to make sure the test fixturing and procedures were safe. He also planned to implement a safety training program, with classes to be taught by different members of the group. It seemed like a straightforward and easily implementable solution.

Bob looked at his group again. Obviously, they did not share his views. "I don't understand your objections," he said to Rod.

"Well, maybe if you'd been in the test lab longer you would," Rod said.

"Wait a minute," Bob said, his voice rising. "I don't think it's a question of seniority. I get paid to make decisions, and it's my decision that we have to do this. If that bothers you, then so be it. We can't keep having these accidents, and 'We'll try harder' isn't an acceptable solution to the problem."

Bob went ahead and made the reviews mandatory, and implemented the safety training program. Other managers in the engineering department (those supported by Bob's group) objected vehemently to the reviews, and regarded them as an infringement of their management charter. The first three safety classes were very poorly prepared and presented. On the day the fourth class was to be presented, the technician scheduled to present it called in sick. That wasn't Bob's biggest problem, though. On that same day, the Test Department's second resignation in as many weeks was submitted, and Bob's boss relieved him of his management responsibilities.

***

By its very nature, business is a competitive and often complex endeavor. To make the business successful, managers must constantly be aware of the environment in which they operate, and make appropriate change. Opportunities, constraints, and threats are imposed by customers, employees, suppliers, competitors, unions, and other internal and external influences. To remain competitive in this complex environment, managers must be able to adapt rapidly, and that requires the ability to recognize the need for and implementation of appropriate change.

A peculiar dichotomy exists here, though. While the need for change is key to the survival of a business, resistance to change is prevalent, and is one of the toughest problems you will ever face as a manager. People just seem to naturally resist change. To further compound the problem, studies have shown that when change is poorly managed, it can cause irreversible damage. This damage can include loss of productivity, morale, motivation, and personnel.

Fortunately, however, effectively managed change can also provide enormous benefits. The obvious benefit is responsiveness to a shifting business environment. In addition to this benefit, well managed change can produce remarkable productivity and morale improvements.

While resistance to change can never be completely eliminated, it can be effectively managed. In order to better understand how to do this, one needs to first examine why resistance to change exists.

RESISTANCE TO CHANGE

People resist change for two reasons. Change is often perceived to be a threat, and detailed knowledge about the change is frequently not made available. Both of these reasons fuel uncertainties about the future.

Change can be threatening for many reasons. One of the most common is insecurity. Change, particularly if it is directed from above, often carries a subtle message:

> "Things have not been quite right in this area, and that's why we are changing the environment in which you must operate."

To an insecure person, that message can be quite threatening.

Change also threatens the ability to control one's environment, particularly when the change is directed from above. As was explained in Chapter 10, in most organizations an informal organization exists along with the formal organization. Subordinates (not managers) design and control the informal organization, and they will work vigorously to maintain it. When a proposed change threatens the informal organization, subordinates naturally also feel threatened. When one realizes that most work gets done through the informal organization, the reasons to minimize perturbations to it are obvious.

Incompetent people are probably threatened more by change than others. Feelings of insecurity often underlie incompetence, which further exacerbates the threatening aspects of change. Incompetent people have usually attained a feeling of equilibrium prior to the change (that is, a state in which their incompetence is masked by the existing order of things). Change of any sort naturally threatens this equilibrium.

Finally, some of the individuals who were doing well prior to the initiation of a change will feel threatened. Again, this feeds on feelings of insecurity. If a new manager takes over the company, people who had advanced as a result of a good personal relationship with the outgoing manager will wonder if they will be able to establish similar relationships with the new manager. If a change in the business environment causes the company to shift its emphasis from new product development to strong financial controls, the people in engineering will feel threatened. According to R. M. Kanter, a consultant specializing in change management, organizational anxieties induced by a fear of reorganizations and mergers now surpass all other sources of career anxiety. The natural reaction is to wonder if things will go as well after the change as before. Since the answer may be no, the change will be resisted.

The other category of reasons for resistance to change is centered around a lack of knowledge concerning the need for change. Kanter suggests that the best way to control this anxiety and resistance to change is to keep everyone who could potentially be affected by the change informed. Our experience indicates that this is a good idea whenever change of any type is introduced.

To take a simple example, suppose your company experiences a drop in sales, which necessitates a cut in the overhead budget. This may make it necessary to eliminate individual subscriptions to newspapers and other professional publications. If the staff members were unaware of the drop in sales and the subsequent need for overhead expense reductions, they would probably feel management was simply being cheap. If the staff understood why the budget reductions were being made, the change would probably be more readily accepted. Cost reductions would probably be even more acceptable to the organization if the members affected by such reductions had a hand in establishing how costs might be reduced, instead of management simply directing the cancellation of all magazine and newspaper subscriptions.

A STRATEGY FOR MANAGING CHANGE

Two underlying themes form the cornerstones for an effective change management approach:

- making the need for change understood, and
- making the change less threatening

With this in mind, the approach can be expanded to a six-step process, as shown in Figure 17–1:

IDENTIFY THE NEED FOR CHANGE

Change should be initiated in response to inabilities or inefficiencies in meeting organizational requirements. If the requirements are not being met, the people who are responsible for meeting them need to be made aware of that fact. Unnecessary change is probably one of the more frustrating things managers and subordinates have to deal with in the business environment. If the individuals affected by change are unaware of the reasons why change is needed, it is easy to assume the change is frivolous. The need for change has to be real, and it has to be known to those it will affect. We've found that one of the best ways to identify the need for change and simultaneously get a head start on communicating information about the change is to enlist the assistance of the people who will be affected by the change. In order to enlist this assistance, though, one needs to first determine who will be affected.

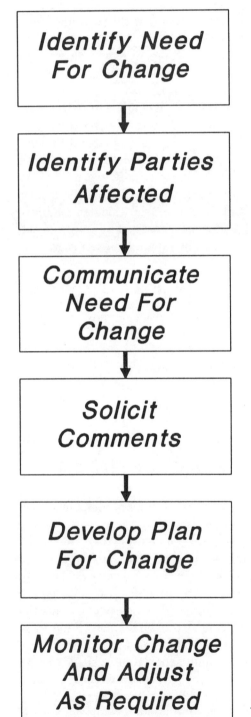

Figure 17–1. *A six-step process for managing change effectively.*

IDENTIFY AFFECTED PARTIES

Identifying the people who will be affected by change is perhaps the easiest part of the change management process. Start with the reasons why change is necessary. Is the accounting department not providing information to your group in a timely manner? If so, personnel from the accounting department will obviously be affected. Is the accounting department's delinquency caused by someone else not getting the right data to them in a timely manner? If so, then these people will also probably be affected.

COMMUNICATE THE NEED FOR CHANGE

Once all parties potentially affected by the change arc identified, a meeting to discuss the need for change is in order. Some judgment will be required here, particularly when dealing with larger groups (for example, a general manager would probably not convene all employees to discuss potential changes to the retirement plan). As a new manager, though, you would probably do well by convening all of the people in your group (as well as appropriate representatives from other affected groups) to discuss the need for change. This need should be identified in clear and nonthreatening language. Explain the reasons why you believe change is required, but keep it nonpersonal. Don't identify what the change will be, only that change is required to better allow your group to meet its commitments.

At the same time you meet with these people, it would be a good idea to ask them who else might be affected. Initially, you may not want to meet with everyone. For example, if it appears a termination might be a necessary part of the change, you probably would not want to include the person likely to be terminated. In most cases, though, you should meet with everyone, or representatives of everyone, who will be affected. This is important, because it greatly enhances the probability that all objections to any proposed change will become known, and if you know about the objections, you can take steps to alleviate them.

SOLICIT COMMENTS

After the need for change has been identified by the group, ask for their help. If you ask for assistance in identifying what the change could be, and how it might be effectively implemented, you will reap several rewards. You and the people affected by the change will probably develop better ideas than you would if you were working alone. Making the affected people part of the solution (instead of part of the problem) will establish a sense of ownership in the development of the change. The group will more readily accept the change, and find it to be less threatening.

In many cases, you may still encounter resistance from some group members. Don't be threatened by this resistance, and don't show emotion or dismiss the reasons for their resistance as trivial. If you let the people who object have their say, other group members may develop counter-arguments without your intervention. This will strengthen the group's recognition of the need for change. If the person objects to the need for change with generalities, push for specifics, and listen to what is said. There may be valid reasons why a change is unwise.

DEVELOP A PLAN FOR THE CHANGE

After identifying a need for change and soliciting comments from the right people, you will be well prepared to start thinking about how best to implement the change. As a result of soliciting their comments, you know what the objections will be, and you may even have recommendations to overcome the objections. You now need to review the requirements for change, and determine if they can be satisfied while simultaneously incorporating the group's comments.

Considerable judgment will be required in this area. You may be able to satisfy all requirements and incorporate all of the group's recommendations. This usually doesn't happen, though, and you will have to make some compromises. If you can legitimately postpone some of the necessary changes in order to meet the group's objections, we recommend that you do so. This will show the group that you are responsive to their concerns, and help to assure acceptance of the change. You won't be able to compromise on every issue, but if you do so wherever possible, you will come out ahead. In addition to considering all of the affected parties' recommendations, it's a good idea to consider incrementally introducing the change. This may further mitigate any resistance.

An important part of the planning process is risk assessment. Many of the risks inherent to the change will have been identified by you and the other affected parties, but there will probably be other risks.

Identifying these additional risks requires an application of the techniques to be discussed later in Chapter 19, as well as other considerations. For example, if the change is absolutely necessary but one or more people are very opposed to it, how will the group's morale be affected? Will the group continue to meet its commitments? What if the people who object resign, or seek a transfer? All of these factors need to be considered, and appropriate responses developed prior to initiating the change. As risks are identified, you may want to modify the implementation plan, and consider any new risks the modified plan presents.

MONITOR CHANGE AND ADJUST AS REQUIRED

Once implementation of the change is underway, monitor progress against the change implementation plan closely. Check with your people and others frequently to identify any problems. If unforeseen problems develop, modify the plan accordingly. Inputs from the people closest to the change will provide the most usable information, but once again, all people affected by the change should be consulted.

CONCLUSIONS

As stated at the beginning of this chapter, resistance to change is one of the toughest problems a manager will face. The problem is even more acute for young or new managers. That's because older or more experienced employees will be even more likely to question the need for any change.

The two dominant reasons people resist change are because the need for change is not well understood, and because change is threatening. The strategy for effectively managing change outlined in this chapter focuses on overcoming those two factors by clearly identifying the reason for change, and actively involving the parties affected in the change. While this strategy will not totally eliminate resistance to change (we don't believe resistance to change can be totally eliminated), it will reduce resistance to a point where it does not interfere with the ability of your group to meet its commitments.

Further Reading

Parson, Mary Jean, "Making Changes: How to Budge the Office Mule," *Working Woman*, September 1987.

Ward, Bernie, "Managing Change," *Sky*, July 1987.

Kanter, Rosabeth Moss, "Managing Traumatic Change: Avoiding the Unlucky 13," May 1987.

Bridges, William, "Managing Organizational Transitions," *Organizational Dynamics*, 1986.

Chapter 18
MANAGING CONFLICT

Of the many challenges faced by new managers, one of the most difficult is managing conflict. Conflict appears to represent exactly the opposite of what most of us want, and that's a smooth-running, efficient organization. Conflict seems to suggest that things are not quite right, and by implication, that your group is not as well managed as it should be.

All business organizations operate in a changing environment, however, and changing environments require the business to be adaptive. If the business is not adaptive, it will soon be noncompetitive, and noncompetitive businesses don't survive.

In truth, some kinds of conflict are a good thing, and a sign of a healthy organization. The members of growing, developing organizations are always creating new ideas to make things better. These ideas will be different, and they will have to compete for resources. Some conflict is a natural by-product of this process. Discussion, disagreement, and even arguments are often necessary to identify all options in response to business problems, and then to select and refine the best option.

On the other hand, there are types of conflict that impede getting the job done. In these situations, conflicts between individuals may prevent them from working together. In some cases, this feeling can extend to envelop entire organizations, pitting one group against another. If the groups have to work together, the larger business organization suffers.

Perhaps the best way to begin a discussion on how to manage conflict is with a definition. Verderber and Verderber of the University of Cincinnati define conflict as "the clash of opposing attitudes, ideas, behaviors, goals, and needs." Note that this definition contains elements that can pertain to personal issues (value conflicts between individuals), as well as substantive issues (disagreements about nonpersonal issues, or issues of substance). Recognizing this distinction will help to understand how to manage conflict. Separating the personal and substantive elements of a conflict and then focusing on the substantive issues is an important key to successful conflict resolution. An example will help to illustrate this point.

George and Ed sell stocks for a financial services company, with the majority of their sales being conducted over the telephone. Both report to the same supervisor, Joe. Ed recently was promoted to the next higher salary grade and received a modest salary increase. George was not promoted, but his responsibilities shifted. Instead of selling by telephone to individual investors, George was reassigned to institutional investors (i.e., pension fund and other financial organizations that trade stocks in larger quantities).

Prior to George's shift in responsibilities and Ed's promotion, both men worked in partitioned cubicles. After Ed's promotion, he kept his cubicle office. George (who was not promoted) moved into a larger office with a window and a door.

Joe (the supervisor) noticed that the relationship between the two men began to deteriorate. Ed developed a surly attitude, both toward George and Joe. One day George and Ed had an embarrassingly loud argument. Up to that time, Joe ignored the increasingly obvious conflict between the two men. Things had reached a point, however, where he could no longer do so.

Joe called both men into his office and asked them what the argument was about. Ed accused George of "acting like a prima donna," and "using a disproportionately large portion of the overhead budget for telephone bills." George explained that even though he wasn't selling on the telephone anymore, he couldn't operate on the small telephone budget he had. Joe started to ask George for more information, but Ed (who was obviously emotionally distraught) walked out of the meeting.

Both Joe and George were surprised. "What's going on here, George?" Joe asked.

"I really don't know," George answered. "Ever since you promoted Ed, he's been acting like a horse's ass."

Joe waited until later in the day to see Ed. "Let's get a cup of coffee, Ed," Joe said, and the two men went to a break area. After some small talk, Joe said "Care to tell me what's going on?"

"Well," Ed said, "I think he should cut back on his telephone expenses now that he's not in direct sales anymore." Ed continued talking, and Joe listened. When Ed finished, Joe took another sip of coffee.

"You're probably right, Ed, but people normally don't almost get into fist fights over something that trivial. What's really going on?"

Ed sat silent for a long time. Finally he said "How come I get promoted and I'm still stuck in a cubicle, while he gets a fancy office without getting promoted?"

Joe nodded his head. "Okay, I see your point. Let me see if I can explain. George deals with people face-to-face, not over the telephone, like you do. You're one of our best telephone account executives. George is better face-to-face. He doesn't have your telephone sales skills, and it was showing in his sales figures. That's why he didn't get promoted this year, and you did.

"When George's customers come in, though, he can't sell to them if he's in a cubicle. He and they need a private place, and that's why he has a walled office, with a door."

Ed's attitude began to change soon after the meeting, and the conflict softened. Within a few days, the two men were working together as well as they had before the conflict began.

Joe used several conflict management skills to bring this about. At first, he ignored the conflict. This is frequently, at least initially, the best approach. That's because people will often resolve conflicts themselves without management intervention, and waiting to see if this will occur both eases the management burden and establishes ownership (on the part of the conflicting individuals) in the resolution. The key to doing this successfully is knowing when to intervene. If the conflict is counterproductive or escalates into overt hostility, or simply goes on too long (and you have to be the judge of this), management intervention is required. Joe recognized this to be the case when George and Ed began to argue loudly. Even though Ed left in a huff, the initial approach of talking to both conflicting parties simultaneously is a good one. This avoids any appearance of favoritism.

Joe's next move was to wait until later in the day before speaking with Ed again. When someone becomes emotionally overwrought and behaves in an unreasonable manner like Ed did, waiting is usually the best approach. Unreasonable behavior is just that, and when a person behaves irrationally, attempting to persuade or even communicate is a futile gesture.

Finally, when Joe met with Ed later in the day, he did so over a cup of coffee in a nonthreatening environment. During this meeting, Joe exercised perhaps the most critical conflict management skill. He allowed Ed to initially focus on the personal aspects of the conflict, but then pressed for the *substantive* issues. Ed finally admitted that it was George's fancier office that bothered him, and Joe was able to explain why. After that, the conflict dissolved.

The above example is a fairly simple application of a few basic conflict management skills. Other conflict management skills are discussed below, but before attempting to apply these skills, one must first determine if eliminating the conflict is desirable, and this requires determining if the conflict is productive or not. If the conflict does not hurt productivity or morale, leave the situation alone (in fact, conflict may introduce an element of competition, which often improves both productivity and morale). If productivity or morale goes down (as is likely the case if the conflict is personal), you need to take action.

PERSONAL CONFLICT

In some cases, conflict between individuals is purely personal. Personal conflict can exist between individuals or groups. The distinguishing characteristic of personal conflict is that it is based largely on negative feelings about the other individual or group, and less on factual or substantive issues. In other words, the parties involved in a personal conflict simply dislike each other or the members of the other group. Sources of personal conflict can be deep-rooted feelings, standards of conduct, values, business philosophies, or other intangible factors. Personal conflict is always bad, but there are ways to manage it.

The first step in dealing with personal conflict is to meet with the people involved. Most people are smart enough to recognize that the ability to get along with others is a key factor in determining continuing employment and future advancement. The fact that a manager called two conflicting individuals in to discuss the conflict should, in itself, encourage them to resolve their differences. If the two agree to work together, leave things alone, but continue to quietly monitor the situation.

If the conflicting individuals are unwilling to resolve their differences (and this will be apparent rather quickly), you have several other options. If it's important that the two continue to work on the same project, you might modify the work flow to use a third person as a go-between, or buffer. Sometimes simply changing the office arrangement to separate the two will help. If keeping them on the same project is not important, reassign one to a different project.

Most of the time, personal conflicts arise between individuals. Sometimes, personal conflicts occur between groups. Such conflicts may be based on substantive issues, but our experience shows that most of the time these issues are so old they no longer matter. In such situations most group members either can't remember what the issues were, or they came into the group after the conflict had begun and never knew the issues. Sometimes group managers have a personal conflict, and the feeling permeates each group. If this is the case, the action for settling individual personal conflicts described above is appropriate.

If the managers work well together, the conflict will be fairly easy to resolve. In such situations, one might wonder why the conflict existed in the first place. The origin of such a conflict can frequently be traced to individuals who are no longer with the group. A good way to resolve this situation is to orchestrate a project that requires both groups to work together. We've seen situations in which this approach causes conflicts to disappear almost immediately.

SUBSTANTIVE CONFLICT

Substantive conflict is based primarily on disagreement over factual (or substantive) issues. The sources of substantive conflict may be allocation of resources, different organizational preferences, different priorities, or other reasons. Purely substantive individual conflicts are not common. By the time such conflicts come to your attention, they will probably have developed personal overtones. The good news, though, is that substantive conflicts are rooted in nonpersonal issues, and since only factual issues are involved, purely substantive conflicts are usually easier to resolve than personal conflicts.

One method of resolution is for you to meet with the conflicting individuals. The issues are identified by each person, along with their recommendations for resolution. The individuals will often resolve the issues by themselves, with you acting more as a facilitator than an arbitrator. We believe this occurs because it's usually the first time each party hears the other person's views.

Another approach we favor is to first ask the conflicting parties to attempt a compromise by themselves, with the understanding that you will become involved only if they cannot agree. This technique is often successful. It also has another advantage: It develops the ability to resolve conflicts without involving the boss.

Purely substantive conflicts between groups are somewhat more common than those between individuals, probably because individuals in the group don't take such conflicts as personal challenges. Accordingly, such conflicts are fairly easy to settle. If the conflict is between your group and another, a good first step is to examine the conflict from the other group's perspective. This will help to identify the problems being experienced by the other group and will probably lead you to think of an intelligent compromise to offer.

The next step should be a meeting between you and the manager of the other group. It's very important that you not be emotional in this meeting. Focus on the issues in a calm and deliberate manner. Begin the meeting by explaining the problems faced by your group and how these problems created the conflict, and then ask the other manager to do the same. Listen carefully to what the other manager has to say. Even though you attempted to identify the other manager's concerns beforehand, you may be surprised at his or her views, and see things in a new light.

If the other manager's description of the issues agrees closely with what you predicted, recommend the compromises you developed. If the other manager's perceptions are different from your own, modify your suggestions accordingly. Be prepared to concede on a few issues. Standing on principle is not productive if you can work out a solution that benefits both groups.

In most cases, conflicts will be a mixture of personal and substantive conflicts for both individuals and groups (our experience shows that this is nearly always true). To manage these conflicts, you must first separate the personal issues from the substantive ones, and then deal with each separately (as did Joe, when dealing with the conflict between George and Ed in our example).

This is frequently a difficult thing to do. People tend to mask personal conflicts with substantive issues, and substantive issues frequently lead to personal conflicts. In other words, if individuals or groups have a personal conflict, they will find substantive issues about which they can disagree. The only solution is persistence in continuing the effort to get at the root causes of the conflict.

CONCLUSIONS

When managed effectively, conflict can be a very positive thing. In fact, the absence of conflict usually indicates a stagnant, decaying organization. Instead of fearing conflict, you should welcome it. When managed effectively, conflict frequently surfaces the real issues, and that leads to innovation, improved working relationships, and a more efficient organization. The key to successful conflict management is recognizing the two forms of conflict (personal and substantive), and persistently working to peel the personal issues away from the substantive ones. When purely personal conflicts cannot be resolved, the use of performance counselling, buffers, reassignment, or physical separation can often diminish any interference with work group output. Our experience shows, however, that these management actions are more the exception than the rule if the approach suggested in this chapter is followed.

Further Reading

Verderber, Rudolph and Kathleen, *Interact*, University of Cincinnati, Wadsworth Publishing Company, 1980.

Parson, Mary Jean, "Creating Solutions, Not Showdowns," *Working Woman*, May 1987.

Francis, Philip H., *Principles of R&D Management*, Amacom, 1977.

Chapter 19
MANAGING RISK

One of the principal functions of a manager is to control risk. We've all heard comments like "it's a calculated risk" or "the odds are pretty good." Most of the time people making these statements are doing so very casually. Have you ever seen their calculations, or do you think they knew what the odds really were?

This chapter is not intended to tax your abilities as a statistician, although many people think that's what risk management is all about. The philosophy of risk management, for the most part, is not quantitative. Our purpose in this final chapter is to acquaint you with this philosophy, and discuss methods for managing risk effectively.

There are many definitions of risk. The dictionary defines it as exposure to loss or harm. We've also seen risk defined as the probability of loss multiplied by the magnitude of the loss. Still another definition of risk defines it as uncertainty, and in particular, the uncertainty associated with meeting all requirements. All of these are valid concepts, and will fall in place as we continue our discussion. For the time being, though, let's stick with the simplest definition, and call risk exposure to loss or harm.

RISK MANAGEMENT

Risk may be associated with financial or legal affairs, the reputation of your company, product quality, delivery schedule, safety, or a host of other issues. Let's think about this another way. Consider one of your major projects, and imagine a year has gone by. Think about the major problems you will be facing. If the project is a production program, you will probably be very concerned with delivery schedules. If you are launching a new advertising campaign, the effectiveness of the advertising on the target market will be of primary concern. If it's the design of a new product, you may be faced with performance or testing issues. If you work in a small accounting company and you land a major new customer, you will probably be concerned about the ability of your company to meet the new customer's requirements. Whatever problems you anticipate facing in a year, what are the things you should be doing today to minimize or prevent these problems from developing?

This is the essence of risk management, which is really nothing more than a common-sense approach to understanding requirements, identifying the problems likely to be associated with meeting these requirements, and taking appropriate actions to control this risk.

The process can be expanded to include the following four steps (illustrated in Figure 19–1):

- Define the requirements
- Identify the risks
- Eliminate or minimize the risks
- Decide what to do about the remaining risks

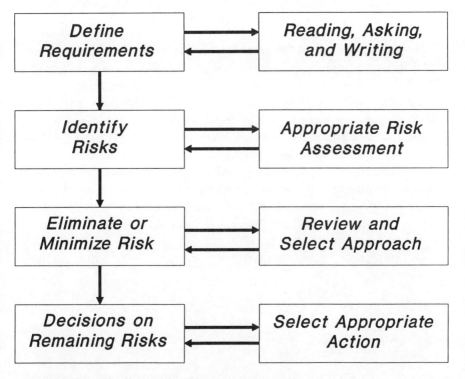

Figure 19–1. The risk management process.

DEFINE THE REQUIREMENTS

We believe this area gives more trouble than any other. If you don't think so, consider these examples:

Have you ever worked on a project in which your team overlooked a minor requirement, and the oversight became a major problem (perhaps even a show-stopper)? We know of a person who wanted to open a gun store and had secured all of the necessary federal, state, and local permits, but had failed to install a burglar detection system required by the local police department. Opening the store for business was delayed for nearly five weeks as the owner searched for, selected, and finally installed a system meeting the police department's requirements.

Has your company ever had to shut down until the plant was brought into compliance with an obscure environmental regulation? This happened to a manufacturing company we once worked with, when a state environmental agency closed the factory because it used a painting process that emitted too many volatile fumes.

Have you ever lost an important sale because you didn't understand all of the customer's requirements? We know of a defense contractor that lost money on a major contract and infuriated a purchasing agency of the US Army when it continually delivered late data, primarily because the contractor didn't understand the magnitude of the job when initially bidding the contract. Ultimately, the Army cancelled the contract and went to a competitor.

Defining all the requirements should be the first step of any venture, be it a new program, design of a new product, or the initiation of a new manufacturing process. These requirements may come from many sources: customers, federal, state, and local laws, internal company standards, and public image.

Defining these requirements involves three efforts: reading, asking, and writing:

Reading. Review every document associated with the effort you manage. These documents will contain requirements that cannot be (but often are) overlooked.

Asking. Ask experts in other areas of your company to identify requirements that may affect the projects you manage. Most companies have legal, environmental, safety, and public relations experts. These experts are valuable sources of information, and can identify requirements that might otherwise go unknown until it's too late.

Writing. Keep a list of the requirements and make sure everyone complies with them. It's not unusual for some projects to have hundreds or even thousands of requirements. Keeping a list assures that you won't forget any.

IDENTIFY THE RISKS

There are three areas to which risk identification can be applied:

- Programs
- Procedures
- Products

Of the many risk analysis techniques, we've found one that is particularly well-suited for program risk identification, and another that is similarly useful for procedure risk identification. Product risk identification is more complex, and usually requires technical assistance.

PROGRAM RISKS

Our favorite technique for identifying program risk is yes-no analysis. Yes-no analysis is a graphical approach to identifying all program elements, and determining if each can be accomplished. We'll develop this concept with two examples, a simple one at first, and then a more complex effort.

For the first project, suppose you manage a computer group responsible for providing computer services to the rest of a larger company. One of the other department managers has asked you to purchase the best data base management software package. The yes-no analysis starts by identifying the top-level output of the project. In this case, its selecting and purchasing the best data base management program to meet the needs of the department manager, as is shown in the top block of Figure 19–2. Intuitively, you feel you can do this job because you've purchased other software programs, but since you've never purchased a data base management system, a "no" is put in the top block.

Even though you've never purchased a data base management system, though, you know the steps you must go through in order to make an intelligent choice. You need to define the department manager's requirements, review available software packages to determine which ones meet those requirements, and make a decision based on meeting the requirements at the lowest cost. Each of these tasks are sub-elements, and are drawn in blocks on the tier below the top block. Since you know that you can do each of the sub-elements, each is labelled "yes," and because all of the sub-elements can be done, the top block moves from a "no" to a "yes." The conclusion of this yes-no analysis is that the project can be accomplished, and entails little risk.

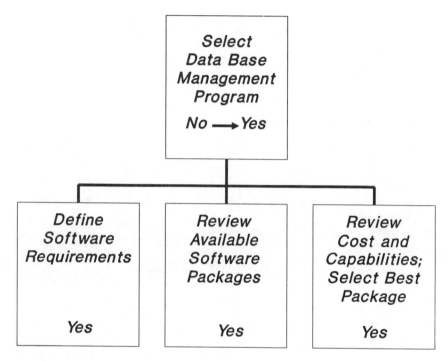

Figure 19–2. Yes-No analysis for selection and purchase of a data base management system.

Let's now move to a more complex example. Suppose you work for a hazardous waste disposal company, and you have been asked to examine the feasibility of building a toxic dump site in Beverly Hills. As shown in Figure 19–3, the top block contains a description of the program output, "Build Hazardous Waste Facility in Beverly Hills." You don't know at this point if you can build such a facility, especially in a community as prestigious as Beverly Hills. That's why there's a "no" in this block.

A "no" in a block doesn't necessarily mean you should abandon the project. You need to identify what makes the block a "no." Some of the sub-elements are labelled "yes," and some are labelled "no." The tasks in those blocks labelled "yes" are ones you are sure you can accomplish. You are not certain, though, about the blocks labelled "no."

The analysis continues in this fashion, with each "no" block being further developed to identify its sub-elements (and determine which ones cause the next higher block to be a "no"). In some cases, a "no" block will become a "yes" if all identified sub-elements are labelled "yes" (for example, see the block labelled "Buy Land"). In other cases, a

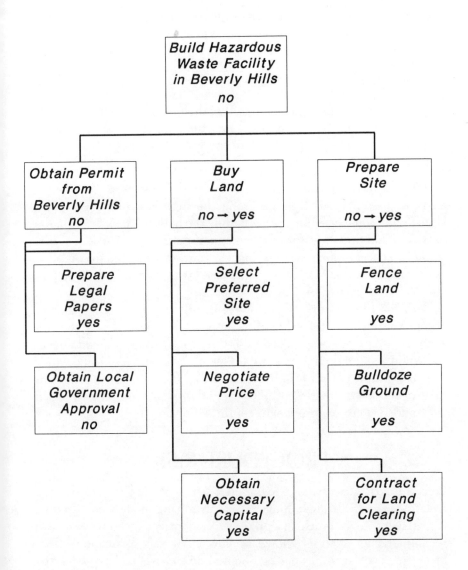

Figure 19–3. Yes-no analysis for building a hazardous waste facility in Beverly Hills.

"no" block will remain a "no" (see the block labelled "Obtain permit from Beverly Hills").

Each "no" block is an important output of risk identification analysis, because these blocks identify the tasks that present the most uncertainty. If you decide to go ahead with a project, schedule all tasks identified as "nos" as early as possible. Why? Because the following is an all-too-common complaint:

> "It seems like we spend 90 percent of the budget to complete the first 90 percent of the program, and then we spend another 90 percent over budget to complete the last 10 percent of the program. . . ."

We all have a natural tendency to delay difficult tasks. A "yes-no" analysis prevents this by identifying the high risk tasks. With this knowledge, a manager can then schedule the high risk tasks early in the program, and prevent throwing good money after bad. The idea is that if you can't accomplish the "no" blocks, you won't be able to complete the program. If that's going to be the case, you want to find out before you've spent most of your money.

Let's put this in perspective by returning to our hypothetical hazardous waste site in Beverly Hills. Suppose, after completing the risk analysis, we decide to proceed with the project. As explained above, we would want to do the "nos" first. One of the blocks identified with a "no" is "Obtain Permit from Beverly Hills." It makes sense to do this first, because we wouldn't want to expend resources on other things if we couldn't get city approval to continue the project.

PROCEDURE RISK

Procedure risk assessment techniques are designed to identify the risks associated with such things as manufacturing sequences, administrative work-flows, or use of a product. To identify procedure risks, we recommend an analysis known as flow chart risk assessment. This technique consists of preparing detailed flow charts and assessing the consequences of missed steps, out-of-sequence steps, or improperly performed steps. The analysis of each step in the flow chart is best presented in a tabular format, with one page devoted to each step.

To illustrate the concept, consider a procedure for preparing and submitting requests for money to purchase new office furniture. Figure 19–4 shows a flow chart for this procedure, and Figure 19–5 shows the tabular analysis associated with one of the steps.

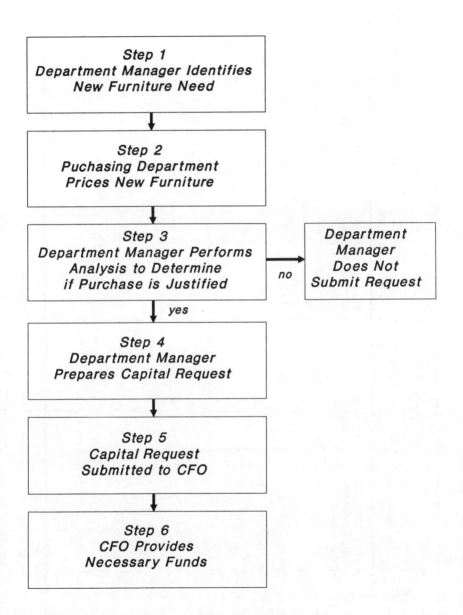

Figure 19–4. Risk assessment for a capital expenditure.

| Step | Consequences Of: | | | Recommendations |
	Missed Step	Out-Of-Sequence Step	Improperly-Performed Step	
Step 4. Department Manager Performs Financial Analysis To Determine If Purchase Is Justified.	May Purchase Unnecessary Furniture.	No Impact.	May Purchase Unnecessary Furniture, Or Not Purchase Necessary Furniture, Depending On Direction Of Error.	Recommend Second Independent Review Of Financial Analysis To Justify Furniture Purchase.

Figure 19–5. One-step analysis.

In the flow shown in this example, there is no further check once the department manager has approved the purchase. The flow chart risk assessment points up the importance of accurate financial analysis. It also recommends an additional check to assure that the analysis is correct.

PRODUCT RISK

Product risk analyses determine if a new product can meet all requirements. These include such things as performance, safety, reliability, quality, cost, or aesthetic requirements. Such analyses often require specialized training, and they should be done by your company' engineering department or by outside consultants. Even though product risk assessments are complex, the questions they answer are simple. These questions concern how the product could fail, be improperly used, or otherwise not meet requirements. Children's toys are good examples of products that could very easily be used improperly, with potentially disastrous consequences (examples include toys that are small enough to swallow, or that have sharp edges). At the other end of the spectrum, consider the ill-fated Challenger space shuttle. Obviously, the rocket motors' failure modes did not receive adequate attention during their design. Whatever the nature of your business, you provide a product of some kind (even in a service industry). As a manager, you should make sure the questions raised here have been addressed, and that assessments have been prepared to identify the risk associated with each product requirement.

ELIMINATE OR MINIMIZE THE RISKS

Eliminating or minimizing seems a logical next step. Even it has subtleties, though. Suppose you find a hazardous design feature. You can:

- add features to warn of the risk;
- train people to avoid injury;
- redesign the product to eliminate the hazard.

Of the three methods, the third is preferred. It eliminates the risk entirely. The other two are less desirable because they depend on freedom from human error, which is much less certain.

The same approach holds true for procedure or process risks. Procedure risk involves only two choices. Eliminating risks by changing the procedure is preferable to special reminders. The procedure should be redesigned to minimize the susceptibility to human error.

Program risk is somewhat different, in that programs usually cannot be "redesigned" to eliminate or minimize risk. However, program requirements can be changed or the schedule can be modified to do the least certain projects first (as in yes-no analysis).

DECIDE WHAT TO DO ABOUT THE REMAINING RISK

Once you have defined the requirements, identified the risks, and eliminated or minimized as much risk as possible, the next step is to examine the remaining risk and decide what to do about it. Keep in mind that the greater the risk, the more detailed the examination should be. Once you have done this, you have to decide what to do about the remaining risks.

Go with the Risk. You, your boss, or the top management of your company may decide to accept the risk. For example, the risk may be acceptable if it has a low probability of occurrence or the consequences are not disastrous.

Share the Risk. It may be possible to share the risk. For example, automobile manufacturers share repair-cost risk with their customers by imposing time and mileage limitations on new car warranties. They also share risk with their suppliers by issuing separate tire and battery warranties.

Transfer the Risk. Transferring the risk is commonly done through insurance. This is usually done if the probability of occurrence is low, but the consequences are severe (fire and flood insurance are good examples).

Give Up. After completing the first three steps of the risk management process, you may find that the remaining risk is too severe or likely, and it cannot be shared or transferred. Here's where the definition of risk being equal to the probability of the risk times the cost associated with the risk (mentioned at the beginning of this chapter) comes into play. Obviously, a risk that has a moderate to high probability of occurrence and unacceptably catastrophic consequences should not be accepted. In these instances, declining to participate in the venture is the smart move.

ADVISE AND RECOMMEND

Whatever conclusions you reach, it would be prudent to make sure your superiors know what's happening. They will probably want to reserve the decisions for themselves. In that case, make your recommendation on the appropriate course of action. Be sure to identify all of the advantages and disadvantages of your recommendation, and why you selected it over other available options.

References

Anthony, Robert N., and Dearden, John, *Management Control Systems*, Richard D. Irwin, Inc., 1980.

Payne, Thomas A., *Quantitative Techniques for Management*, Reston Publishing Company, Inc., 1982.

Steiner, George A., Miner, John B., and Gray, Edmund R., *Management Policy and Strategy*, Macmillan Publishing Company, Inc., 1982.

Hammer, Willie, *Handbook of System and Product Safety*, Prentice-Hall, Inc., 1972.

Brigham, Eugene F., *Financial Management*, The Dryden Press, 1982.

Roland, Harold E., "Risk Domain of System Safety," *Hazard Prevention*, Vol. No. 22, No. 6, November/December 1986.

INDEX

MANAGING EFFECTIVELY SEMINARS
Available Training Programs

Managing Effectively Seminars training programs are available for in-house presentation. Training programs include Supervision, Planning, Interviewing, Manufacturing Leadership Training, Systems Failure Analysis, Continuous Improvement Implementation, Risk Management, Quality Measurement Systems, Value Improvement, Business and Technical Writing, Design of Experiments, and Drawing Interpretation. Other tailored programs can be developed on short notice to meet client needs. Detailed descriptions of our training programs can be obtained by contacting Managing Effectively Seminars at 909 946-5932.